THE BATTLE OF GETTYSBURG

COLONEL FRANKLIN ARETAS HASKELL

THE BATTLE OF
GETTYSBURG

BY
COLONEL FRANK A. HASKELL
AIDE-DE-CAMP TO GENERAL JOHN GIBBON
AND COLONEL OF THE THIRTY-SIXTH
WISCONSIN INFANTRY

CHAPMAN BILLIES, INC.
SANDWICH, MASSACHUSETTS

This edition first published in 1993 by
Chapman Billies, Inc.
P.O. Box 819
Sandwich, MA 02563

ISBN: 0–939218–12–7

Printed in the United States of America.

Publisher's Note

This edition of Colonel Haskell's account of the Battle of Gettysburg is based on the text which appears in the second edition published by the Wisconsin History Commission in 1910, and which we have edited for spelling and style.

We have omitted the Tribute to Adjutant Haskell by J. A. Watrous.

The amendatory footnotes are from the uncredited edition found on the CD-ROM *Great Literature,* published in 1992 by Bureau Development, Inc.

The frontispiece portrait of Colonel Haskell is taken from the WHC edition, as are the maps on pages 47 and 99. The map on page 8 and the other line drawings and engravings are from *Gettyburg: How the Battle Was Fought,* by Captain James T. Long, Harrisburg: 1891.

—GEORGE DAWSON, Publisher

PREFACE
TO
The First Edition

RANK ARETAS HASKELL was born at Tunbridge, Vermont, the son of Aretas and Ann (Folson) Haskell, on the 13th of July, 1828. Graduating from Dartmouth College with distinguished honors, in the class of 1854, the young man came to Madison, Wisconsin, in the autumn of that year, and entered the law firm of Orton, Atwood & Orton. His career in this profession was increasingly successful, until in 1861 it was interrupted by the outbreak of the War between the States.

Commissioned on June 20th of that year as First Lieutenant of Company I of the Sixth Wisconsin Volunteer Infantry, of the Iron Brigade, he served as Adjutant of his regiment until April 14, 1862. Contemporaneous accounts state that "much of the excellent discipline for which this regiment was distinguished, was due to his soldierly efforts during its organization."

He was called from the adjutancy of the Sixth to be aide-de-camp to General John Gibbon, when the latter assumed command of the Iron Brigade, and remained in such service until (February 9, 1864) he was promoted to be Colonel of the Thirty-sixth Wisconsin. While aide to General Gibbon he was temporarily on the staffs of several other generals, including Edwin V. Sumner and G. K. Warren, and won wide repute as a soldier of unusual ability and courage. With the Iron Brigade, he participated in the campaigns of the Army of the Potomac, taking part in reconnaissances at Orange Court House and Stephensburg, in skirmishes at Rappahannock Station and Sulphur Springs, and in the battles of Gainesville, Second Bull Run, South Mountain, Antietam, Fredericksburg, Chancellorsville, and Gettysburg. Reporting upon the battle of December 13, 1862, at Fredericksburg, General Gibbon alluded to his favorite aide as being "constantly on the field, conveying orders and giving directions amid the heaviest fire."

Writing of Gettysburg, which is herein so graphically depicted by Haskell, General Francis A. Walker, in his *History of the Second Army Corps*,[1] refers to our author as one who was "bravest of the brave, riding mounted through an interval between the Union battalions, and calling upon the troops to go forward." He further says: "Colonel Frank A. Haskell, of Wisconsin, had been known for his intelligence and courage, for his generosity of character and his exquisite culture, long before the third day of Gettysburg, when, acting as aide to General Gibbon, he rode mounted between

---

1. *History of the Second Army Corps in the Army of the Potomac* (New York, 1886), pp. 512, 513

the two lines, then swaying backward and forward under each other's fire, calling upon the men of the Second Division to follow him, and setting an example of valor and self-devotion never forgotten by any man of the thousands who witnessed it."

General Winfield S. Hancock, officially reporting upon the battle, thus alluded to Haskell's deed: "I desire particularly to refer to the services of a gallant young officer, First Lieutenant F. A. Haskell, aide-de-camp to Brigadier General Gibbon, who, at a critical period of the battle, when the contending forces were but fifty or sixty yards apart, believing that an example was necessary, and ready to sacrifice his life, rode between the contending lines with a view of giving encouragement to ours and leading it forward, he being at the moment the only mounted officer in a similar position. He was slightly wounded and his horse was shot in several places."

General Gibbon's report said: "I desire to call particular attention to the manner in which several of the subordinate reports mention the services of my gallant aide, Lieutenant F. A. Haskell, Sixth Wisconsin, and to add my testimony of his valuable services. This young officer has been through many battles, and distinguished himself alike in all by his conspicuous coolness and bravery, and in this one was slightly wounded, but refused to quit the field. It has always been a source of regret to me that our military system offers no plan for rewarding his merit and services as they deserve." In later years, the General again publicly alluded to Haskell's heroic conduct on this field: "There was a young man on my staff who had been in every battle with me and who did more than any other one man to repulse Pickett's assault at Gettysburg and he did the part of a general there."

General William Harrow spoke of Haskell as having "greatly distinguished himself by his constant exertion in the most exposed places."

Colonel Norman J. Hall, of the Michigan Seventh Infantry, and then commanding the Third Brigade, thus referred to the incident: "I cannot omit speaking in the highest terms of the magnificent conduct of Lieutenant Haskell, of General Gibbon's staff, in bringing forward regiments and in nerving the troops to their work by word and fearless example."

Upon receiving an appointment as Colonel of the Thirty-sixth Wisconsin, Haskell returned at once to this state and recruited and organized that regiment for the field. Although his commission was dated from February 9, he was not mustered into service as colonel until March 23. The regiment, which had been assigned to the First Brigade, Second Division of the Second Army Corps, left Madison May 10, and seven days later was acting as reserve during the battle at Spottsylvania. Its experiences thenceforth were of the most active character.

The command went into action at Cold Harbor, Virginia, early in the morning of June 3. The official account of what followed is contained in the report of the State Adjutant General: [2] "The whole line advanced upon the enemy by brigades, in column closed in mass by regiments, the Thirty-sixth being in rear of the brigade. On advancing about three-fourths of a mile across an open field, under a heavy artillery fire, and when within about twenty-five rods of the rebel works, partially protected by the brow of a low hill, the Thirty-sixth was found in the advance, leading the brigade. During the advance, Colonel McKeen,[3] commanding the brigade, was killed when the command devolved upon Colonel Haskell. After a moment's rest, Colonel Haskell, by command of General Gibbon, ordered the brigade forward. The men rose to obey, and were met by a shower of bullets, when the other parts of the line halted. Colonel Haskell surveyed the situation for a moment, as if irresolute; he finally gave the order, 'Lie down, men,' which was at once obeyed. An instant afterwards, he was struck in the head by a rebel bullet, and instantly killed. Thus fell one of Wisconsin's most gallant soldiers, a thorough disciplinarian, and an accomplished scholar."

Colonel Clement E. Warner, then a captain in the Thirty-sixth, but later its major and lieutenant colonel, has left us this report of the battle of Cold Harbor, so far as concerns Colonel Haskell's participation and death:[4]

"Frank A. Haskell was in every respect an ideal soldier, according to the highest and best definition of that term. I

---

2. Annual Report of the Adjutant General of the State of Wisconsin for 1865 (Madison, 1866) pp.510.511.
3. Colonel Harvey Boyd McKeen, of Pennsylvania, commander of the Third Brigade.
4. Columbus (Wisconsin) *Democrat*, May 27, 1895.

think he was by education, experience, association, natural ability, and temperament fully as competent to handle a division as a regiment, and in many respects the higher would seem the more appropriate position for him.

"He rejoined the Army of the Potomac with his regiment, the Thirty-sixth Wisconsin, about the middle of May, 1864, at Spottsylvania. The two armies were joined in a death struggle, which was destined to continue almost uninterruptedly until one was effectually wiped from the face of the earth. June 3 at Cold Harbor, our army was massed by division and in that formation projected upon the fortifications of the enemy. Their line of works was really the outer line of the defenses of Richmond, and were perfectly constructed for defense, and manned by General Lee's army, which when protected by works had thus far been able to successfully withstand General Grant's continuous attacks.

"With the general advance our division moved at daylight for nearly two miles over undulating land, part of the time subject to the fire of the enemy and occasionally protected from it by slight depressions in the land. We moved forward as rapidly as possible, and in thirty minutes were in the immediate presence of the enemy's line and subjected to as murderous a fire as met Pickett's men at the celebrated charge at Gettysburg.

"Colonel Haskell, who was so largely instrumental in saving the day at Gettysburg, now finds his position exactly reversed from what it was on that memorable occasion. Now his men were charging and the enemy on the defense, protected by their works. He was standing nearly in front of the remnant of the Second Division which had thus far pressed forward through the murderous fire, and apparently seeing the hopelessness of further advance, and willing to save this remnant of his men, gave the order, 'Lie down, men,' which was the last order he ever gave. It was promptly obeyed. For an instant it seemed that he was the only man standing, and only for an instant, for as he stood surveying the havoc around him, and glanced toward the enemy's line, he was seen to throw up his arms and sink to the earth, his forehead pierced by a rebel ball. And this was the last of Frank Haskell's consciousness. He had fearlessly and freely given his young life for his country. Nearly 15,000 companions joined him in the sacrifice on that fateful morning, the greatest loss of any single charge in the war."

In his own report of the battle, General Hancock said: "General Tyler was wounded and taken from the field, and the lamented McKeen, after pushing his command as far as his example could urge it, was killed. The gallant Haskell succeeded to the command, but was carried from the field mortally wounded, while making renewed efforts to carry the enemy's works." In a field order, dated September 28, 1864, he further declared, "At Cold Harbor the Colonel of the Thirty-sixth Wisconsin — as gallant a soldier as ever lived — fell dead on the field."

General Gibbon, on receiving the news of the Colonel's death, cried, "My God! I have lost my best friend, and one of the best soldiers in the Army of the Potomac has fallen!"

The late Honorable A. J. Turner, editor of the Portage *State Register,* who was well acquainted with Colonel Haskell, said of him: [5] "While commanding a brigade in the assault upon the enemy's lines at the battle of the Chickahominy, near Richmond, Virginia, on the morning of Friday, the 3rd of June, he was struck in the right temple by a Rebel sharpshooter's bullet and died in about three hours. His body was taken in charge by his young and faithful orderly, John N. Ford, who, though himself wounded in the head and left arm, persevered through all difficulties and brought it home to Portage where, attended by a great concourse of people, it was buried in Silver Lake Cemetery, June 12, 1864."

This story of the Battle of Gettysburg was written by Lieutenant Haskell to his brother, H. M. Haskell of Portage, not long after the contest. It was not intended for publication; but its great merit was at once recognized, and it was offered to Mr. Turner for insertion in his weekly paper. It was, however, too long a document for such purpose. About fifteen years later, it was published by Mr. Turner in a pamphlet of 72 pages, without title page, for private circulation only. The account was widely read by military experts and received much praise for both its literary and its professional merit. The pamphlet having become rare, for the edition was small, was reprinted in 1898 as part of the history of Dartmouth's Class of 1854. Certain omissions and changes were, however, made therein by its editor, Captain Daniel Hall, who was an aide on General Howard's staff; the

5. Columbus (Wisconsin) *Democrat,* May 27, 1895.

reason assigned being, that the account was written so soon after the battle that "although surprisingly accurate in minute details," the author was not fully informed relative to one or two facts which to him seemed to reflect on General Sickles. Captain Hall assumed that were Colonel Haskell now living, he would have justified these omissions. In March, 1908, the Dartmouth College version was reprinted by the Commandery of Massachusetts, Military Order of the Loyal Legion, under the editorship of Captain Charles Hunt.

In deciding to inaugurate its own series of reprints with Colonel Haskell's brilliant paper, the Wisconsin History Commission has, in accordance with its fixed policy, reverted to the original edition, which is here presented entire, exactly as first printed. Whatever might have been the author's later judgment, in the event of his surviving the war, the Commission does not feel warranted in disturbing this original text in the slightest degree—the present being an unexpurgated reprint of a rare and valuable narrative written by a soldier in whose memory Wisconsin feels especial pride.

The Commissioners are grateful to Mrs. W. G. Clough, public librarian of Portage, for the loan of that institution's rare copy of the original, for the purpose of this reprint.

—REUBEN G. THWAITES
Secretary, State Historical Society of Wisconsin
April, 1910

THE BATTLE
OF
GETTYSBURG

Upon the Portage [Wisconsin] Public Library's copy of the original pamphlet edition, Hon. A. J. Turner wrote the following explanatory note:

> The within description of 'The Battle of Gettysburg' was written by Colonel Frank A. Haskell, who was on the staff of General John Gibbon, to his brother at Portage, Wisconsin. It was submitted to me soon after, in the *State Register* office, but its great length rendered its publication in our columns quite impossible. The article was written form 'Head Quarters of the Army of the Potomac,' but bore no date, although it was during the same month as the battle, and was written by Colonel Haskell in the intervals of the march, and was a private letter without design of publication—*A. J. Turner*

THE BATTLE
OF
GETTYSBURG

THE GREAT BATTLE of Gettysburg is now an event of the past. The composition and strength of the armies, their leaders, the strategy, the tactics, the result, of that field are today by the side of those of Waterloo—matters of history. A few days ago these things were otherwise. This great event did not so "cast its shadow before," as to moderate the hot sunshine that streamed upon our preceding march, or to relieve our minds of all apprehension of the result of the second great Rebel invasion of the soil north of the Potomac.

No, not many days since, at times we were filled with fears and forebodings. The people of the country, I suppose, shared the anxieties of the army, somewhat in common with us, but they could not have felt them as keenly as we did. We were upon the immediate theatre of events, as they occurred from day to day, and were of them. We were the army whose province it should be to meet this invasion and repel it; on us was the immediate responsibility for results, most momentous for good or ill, as yet in the future. And so in addition to the solicitude of all good patriots, we felt that our own honor as men and as an army, as well as the safety of the capitol and the country, were at stake.

And what if that invasion should be successful, and in the coming battle, the Army of the Potomac should be overpowered? Would it not be? When our army was much larger than at present—had rested all winter—and, nearly perfect in all its departments and arrangements, was the most splendid army this continent ever saw, only a part of the Rebel force, which it now had to contend with, had defeated it—its leader, rather—at Chancellorsville! Now the Rebel had his whole force assembled, he was flushed with recent victory, was arrogant in his career of unopposed invasion, at a favorable season of the year. His daring plans, made by no unskilled head, to transfer the war from his own to his enemies' ground, were being successful. He had gone a day's march from his front before Hooker moved, or was aware of his departure. Then, I believe, the army in general, both officers and men, had no confidence in Hooker, in either his honesty or ability.

Did they not charge him, personally, with the defeat at Chancellorsville? Were they not still burning with indignation against him for that disgrace? And now, again under his leadership, they were marching against the enemy! And they knew of nothing, short of the providence of God, that could, or would, remove him. For many reasons, during the marches prior to the battle, we were anxious, and at times heavy at heart.

But the Army of the Potomac was no band of school girls. They were not the men likely to be crushed or utterly discouraged by any new circumstances in which they might find themselves placed. They had lost some battles, they had gained some. They knew what defeat was, and what was victory. But here is the greatest praise that I can bestow upon them, or upon any army: With the elation of victory, or the depression of defeat, amidst the hardest toils of the campaign, under unwelcome leadership, at all times, and under all circumstances, they were a reliable army still. The Army of the Potomac would do as it was told, always.

Well clothed, and well fed — there never could be any ground for complaint on these heads — but a mighty work was before them. Onward they moved — night and day were blended — over many a weary mile, through dust, and through mud, in the broiling sunshine, in the flooding rain, over steeps, through defiles, across rivers, over last year's battlefields, where the skeletons of our dead brethren, by hundreds, lay bare and bleaching, weary, without sleep for days, tormented with the newspapers, and their rumors, that the enemy was in Philadelphia, in Baltimore, in all places where he was not, yet these men could still be relied upon, I believe, when the day of conflict should come. *Hæc olim meminisse juvabit.* We did not then know this. I mention them now, that you may see that in those times we had

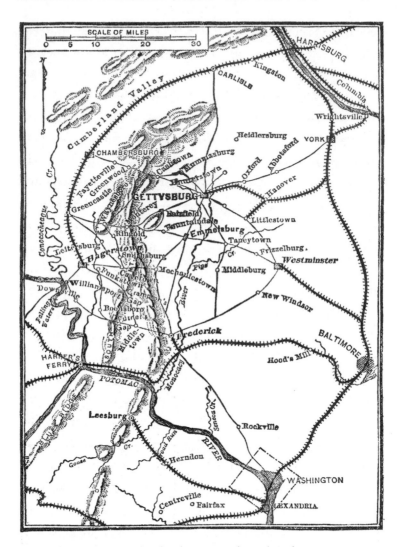

several matters to think about, and to do, that were not as pleasant as sleeping upon a bank of violets in the shade.

In moving from near Falmouth, Virginia, the army was formed in several columns, and took several roads. The

Second Corps, the rear of the whole, was the last to move, and left Falmouth at daybreak, on the 15th of June, and pursued its march through Aquia, Dumfries, Wolf Run Shoales, Centerville, Gainesville, Thoroughfare Gap — this last we left on the 25th, marching back to Haymarket, where we had a skirmish with the cavalry and horse artillery of the enemy — Gum Spring, crossing the Potomac at Edward's Ferry, thence through Poolesville, Frederick, Liberty, and Union Town. We marched from near Frederick to Union Town, a distance of thirty-two miles, from 8:00 A.M. to 9:00 P.M., on the 28th, and I think this is the longest march, accomplished in so short a time, by a corps during the war. On the 28th, while we were near this latter place, we breathed a full breath of joy, and of hope. The Providence of God had been with us — we ought not to have doubted it — General Meade commanded the Army of the Potomac.

Not a favorable time, one would be apt to suppose, to change the general of a large army, on the eve of battle, the result of which might be to destroy the government and country! But it should have been done long before. At all events, any change could not have been for the worse, and the Administration, therefore, hazarded little, in making it now. From this moment my own mind was easy concerning results. I now felt that we had a clear headed, honest soldier, to command the army, who would do his best always — that there would be no repetition of Chancellorsville. Meade was not as much known in the army as many of the other corps commanders, but the officers who knew, all thought highly of him, a man of great modesty, with none of those qualities which are noisy and assuming, and hankering for cheap newspaper fame, not all of the "gallant" Sickles stamp. I happened to know much of General Meade—he and General Gibbon had always been very intimate, and I had seen much of him—I think my own notions concerning General Meade at this time were shared quite generally by the army; at all events, all who knew him shared them.

By this time, by reports that were not mere rumors, we began to hear frequently of the enemy, and of his proximity. His cavalry was all about us, making little raids here and there, capturing now and then a few of our wagons, and stealing a good many horses, but doing us really the least amount possible of harm, for we were not by these means impeded at all, and his cavalry gave no information at all to Lee, that he could rely upon, of the movements of the Army of the Potomac. The Infantry of the enemy was at this time in the neighborhood of Hagerstown, Chambersburg, and some had been at Gettysburg, possibly were there now. Gettysburg was a point of strategic importance, a great many roads, some ten or twelve at least concentrating there, so the army could easily converge

General George Gordon Meade

to, or, should a further march be necessary, diverge from this point. General Meade, therefore, resolved to try to seize Gettysburg, and accordingly gave the necessary orders for the concentration of his different columns there. Under the new auspices the army brightened and moved on with a more elastic step towards the yet undefined field of conflict.

The First Corps (General Reynolds), already having the advance, was ordered to push forward rapidly and take and hold of the town, if he could. The rest of the army would assemble to his support. Buford's Cavalry cooperated with this corps, and on the morning of the 1st of July found the enemy near Gettysburg and to the west, and promptly engaged him. The First Corps having bivouacked the night before, south of the town, came up rapidly to Buford's support, and immediately a sharp battle was opened with the advance of the enemy. The First Division (General Wadsworth) was the first of the infantry to become engaged, but the other two, commanded respectively by Generals Robinson and Doubleday, were close at hand, and forming the line of battle to the west and northwest of the town, at a mean distance of about a mile away, the battle continued for some hours,

General Robert E. Lee

with various success, which was on the whole with us until near noon. At this time a lull occurred, which was occupied, by both sides, in supervising and reestablishing the hastily formed lines of the morning. New divisions of the enemy were constantly arriving and taking up positions, for this purpose marching in upon the various roads that terminate at the town, from the west and north. The position of the First Corps was then becoming perilous in the extreme, but it was improved a little before noon by the arrival upon the field of two divisions of the Eleventh Corps (General Howard), these divisions commanded respectively by Generals Schurz and Barlow, who by order posted their commands to the right of the First Corps, with their right retired, forming an angle with the line of the First Corps. Between 3:00 and 4:00 in the afternoon the enemy, now in overwhelming force, resumed the battle with spirit. The portion of the Eleventh Corps making but feeble opposition to the advancing enemy, soon began to fall back.

Back in disorganized masses they fled into the town, hotly pursued, and in lanes, in barns, in yards and cellars, throwing away their arms, they sought to hide like rabbits, and were there captured, unresisting, by hundreds.

The First Corps, deprived of this support, if support it could be called, outflanked upon either hand, and engaged in front, was compelled to yield the field. Making its last stand upon what is called "Seminary Ridge," not far from the town, it fell back in considerable confusion, through the southwest part of the town, making brave resistance, however, but with considerable loss. The enemy did not see fit to follow, or to attempt to, further than the town, and so the fight of the 1st of July closed here. I suppose our losses during the day would exceed 4,000, of whom a large number were prisoners. Such usually is the kind of loss sustained by the Eleventh Corps. You will remember that the old "Iron Brigade" is in the First Corps, and consequently shared this fight, and I hear their conduct praised on all hands.

In the Second Wisconsin, Colonel Fairchild lost his left arm; Lieutenant Colonel Stevens was mortally wounded, and Major Mansfield was wounded; Lieutenant Colonel Callis, of the Seventh Wisconsin, and Lieutenant Colonel Dudley, of the Nineteenth Indiana, were badly, dangerously wounded, the latter by the loss of his right leg above the knee.

I saw "John Burns," the only citizen of Gettysburg who fought in the battle, and I asked him what troops he fought with. He said: "Oh, I pitched in with them Wisconsin fellers." I asked what sort of men they were, and he answered: "They fit terribly. The Rebs couldn't make anything of them fellers."

And so the brave compliment the brave. This man was touched by three bullets from the enemy, but not seriously wounded.

But the loss of the enemy today was severe also, probably in killed and wounded, as heavy as our own, but not so great in prisoners.

Of these latter, the "Iron Brigade" captured almost an entire Mississippi Brigade, however.

Of the events so far, of the 1st of July, I do not speak from personal knowledge. I shall now tell my introduction to these events.

At 11:00 A.M., on that day, the Second Corps was halted at Taneytown, which is thirteen miles from Gettysburg, South, and there awaiting orders, the men were allowed to make coffee and rest. At between 1:00 and 2:00 in the afternoon, a message was brought to General Gibbon, requiring his immediate presence at the headquarters of General Hancock, who commanded the Corps. I went with General Gibbon, and we rode at a rapid gallop to General Hancock.

At General Hancock's headquarters the following was learned: The First Corps had met the enemy at Gettysburg and had possession of the town. General Reynolds was badly, it was feared mortally, wounded; the fight of the First Corps still continued. By General Meade's order, General Hancock was to hurry forward and take command upon the field, of all troops there, or which should arrive there. The Eleventh Corps was near Gettysburg when the messenger who told of the fight left there, and the Third Corps was marching up, by order, on the Emmetsburg Road—General Gibbon—he was not the ranking officer of the Second Corps after Hancock—was ordered to assume the command of the Second Corps.

All this was sudden, and for that reason, at least, exciting; but there were other elements in this information, that aroused our profoundest interest. The great battle that we had so anxiously looked for during so many days, had at length opened, and it was a relief, in some sense, to have these accidents of time and place established. What would be the result? Might not the enemy fall upon and destroy the First Corps before succor could arrive?

General Hancock, with his personal staff, at about 2:00 P.M., galloped off towards Gettysburg; General Gibbon took his place in command of the Corps, appointing me his acting Assistant Adjutant General. The Second Corps took arms at once, and moved rapidly towards the field. It was not long before we began to hear the dull booming of the guns, and as we advanced, from many an eminence or opening among the trees, we could look out upon the white battery smoke, puffing up from the distant field of blood, and drifting up to the clouds. At these sights and sounds, the men looked more serious than before and were more silent, but they marched faster, and straggled less. At about 5:00 P.M., as we were riding along at the head of the column, we met an ambulance, accompanied by two or three mounted officers — we knew them to be staff officers of General Reynolds — their faces told plainly enough what load the vehicle carried—it was the dead body of General Reynolds. Very early in the action, while seeing personally to the formation of his lines under fire, he was shot through the head by a musket or rifle bullet, and killed almost instantly. His death at this time affected us much, for he was one of the soldier Generals of the army, a man whose soul was in his country's work, which he did with a soldier's high honor and fidelity. I remember seeing him often at the first battle of

Fredericksburg — he then commanded the First Corps — and while Meade's and Gibbon's divisions were assaulting the enemy's works, he was the very beau ideal of the gallant general. Mounted upon a superb black horse, with his head thrown back and his great black eyes flashing fire, he was everywhere upon the field, seeing all things and giving commands in person. He died as many a friend, and many a foe, to the country have died in this war.

Just as the dusk of evening fell, from General Meade, the Second Corps had orders to halt, where the head of the column then was, and to go into position for the night. The Second Division (Gibbon's) was accordingly put in position, upon the left of the Taneytown Road, its left near the southeastern base of Round Top — of which mountain more anon — and the right near the road; the Third Division was posted upon the right of the road, abreast of the Second, and the First Division in the rear of these two — all facing towards Gettysburg.

Arms were stacked, and the men lay down to sleep. Alas! many of them their last but the great final sleep on earth.

Late in the afternoon as we came near the field, from some slightly wounded men we met, and occasional stragglers from the scene of operations in front, we got many rumors and much disjointed information of battle, of lakes of blood, of rout and panic and undescribable disaster, from all of which the narrators were just fortunate enough to have barely escaped, the sole survivors. These stragglers are always terrible liars!

About 9:00 in the evening, while I was yet engaged in showing the troops their positions, I met General Hancock, then on his way from the front, to General Meade, who was back toward Taneytown; and he, for the purpose of having me advise General Gibbon, for his information, gave me quite a detailed account of the situation of matters at Gettysburg, and of what had transpired subsequently to his arrival.

He had arrived and assumed command there, just when the troops of the First and Eleventh Corps, after their repulse, were coming in confusion through the town. Hancock is just the man for such an emergency as this. Upon horseback I think he was the most magnificent looking general in the whole Army of the Potomac at that time. With a large, well-shaped person, always dressed with elegance, even upon that field of confusion, he would look as if he was "monarch of all he surveyed," and few of his subjects would dare to question his right to command, or do aught else but to obey. His quick eye, in a flash, saw what was to be done, and his voice and his royal right hand at once commenced to do it. General Howard had put one of his divisions — Steinwehr — with some batteries, in position, upon a commanding eminence, at the Cemetery, which, as a reserve, had not participated in the fight of the day, and this division was now of course steady. Around this division the fugitives were stopped, and the shattered brigades and regiments, as they returned, were formed upon either flank, and faced toward the enemy again. A show of order at least, speedily came from chaos — the rout was at an end — the First and

Eleventh Corps were in line of battle again—not very systematically formed perhaps—in a splendid position, and in a condition to offer resistance, should the enemy be willing to try them. These formations were all accomplished long before night. Then some considerable portion of the Third Corps (General Sickles) came up by the Emmetsburg Road, and was formed to the left of the Taneytown Road, on an extension of the line that I have mentioned; and all the Twelfth Corps (General Slocum) arriving before night, the divisions were put in position, to the right of the troops already there, to the east of the Baltimore Pike. The enemy was in town, and behind it, and to the east and west, and appeared to be in strong force, and was jubilant over his day's success. Such was the posture of affairs as evening came on of the first of July. General Hancock was hopeful, and in the best of spirits; and from him I also learned that the reason for halting the Second Corps in its present position, was that it was not then known where, in the coming fight, the line of battle would be formed, up near the town, where the troops then were, or further back towards Taneytown. He would give his views upon this subject to General Meade, which were in favor of the line near the town—the one that was subsequently adopted—and General Meade would determine.

The night before a great pitched battle would not ordinarily, I suppose, be a time for much sleep for Generals and their staff officers. We needed it enough, but there was work to be done. This war makes strange confusion of night and day! I did not sleep at all that night. It would, perhaps, be expected, on the eve of such great events, that one should have some peculiar sort of feeling, something extraordinary, some great arousing and excitement of the sensibilities and faculties, commensurate with the event itself; this certainly would be very poetical and pretty, but so far as I was concerned, and I think I can speak for the army in this matter, there was nothing of the kind. Men who had volunteered to fight the battles of the country, had met the enemy in many battles, and had been constantly before them, as had the Army of the Potomac, were too old soldiers and long ago too well had weighed chances and probabilities, to be so disturbed now. No, I believe, the army slept soundly that night, and well, and I am glad the men did, for they needed it.

At midnight General Meade and staff rode by General Gibbon's headquarters, on their way to the field; and in conversation with General Gibbon, General Meade announced that he had decided to assemble the whole army before Gettysburg, and offer the enemy battle there. The Second Corps would move at the earliest daylight, to take up its position.

At 3:00 A.M., of the second of July, the sleepy soldiers of the Corps were aroused; before six the Corps was up to the field, and halted temporarily by the side of the Taneytown Road, upon which it had marched, while some movements of the other troops were being made, to enable it to take position in the order of battle. The morning was thick and sultry, the sky overcast with low, vapory clouds. As we approached, all was astir upon the crests near the Cemetery, and the work of preparation was speedily going on. Men looked like giants there in the mist, and the guns of the frowning batteries so big, that it was a relief to know that they were our friends.

Without a topographical map, some description of the ground and location is necessary to get a clear understanding of the battle. With the sketch I have rudely drawn, without scale or compass, I hope you may understand my description.[1] The line of battle as it was established, on the evening of the first, and morning of the second of July was in the form of the letter "U," the troops facing outwards. And the "Cemetery," which is at the point of the sharpest curvature of the line, being due south of the town of Gettysburg. Round Top, the extreme left of the line, is a small, woody, rocky elevation, a very little west of south of the town, and nearly two miles from it.

The sides of this are in places very steep, and its rocky summit is almost inaccessible. A short distance north of this is a smaller elevation called Little Round Top. On the very top of Little Round Top, we had heavy rifled guns in position during the battle. Near the right of the line is a small, woody eminence, named Culp's Hill. Three roads come up to the town from the south, which near the town are quite straight, and at the town the external ones unite, forming an angle of about sixty, or more degrees. Of these, the farthest

---

1. Colonel Haskell's sketch has not been found; but we have inserted plans of the field, showing the operations of the second and third days—*post*, pp. 47, 99 respectively—ED.

to the east is the Baltimore Pike, which passes by the east
entrance to the Cemetery; the farthest to the west is the
Emmetsburg Road, which is wholly outside of our line of
battle, but near the Cemetery, is within a hundred yards of
it; the Taneytown Road is between these, running nearly due
north and south, by the eastern base of Round Top, by the
western side of the Cemetery, and uniting with the Emmetsburg Road between the Cemetery and the town. High
ground near the Cemetery is named Cemetery Ridge.

The Eleventh Corps (General Howard) was posted at the
Cemetery—some of its batteries and troops actually among
the graves and monuments, which they used for shelter from
the enemy's fire—its left resting upon the Taneytown Road,
extending thence to the east, crossing the Baltimore Pike,
and thence bending backwards towards the southeast; on
the right of the Eleventh came the First Corps, now, since the
death of General Reynolds, commanded by General Newton, formed in a line curving still more towards the South.
The troops of these two corps, were reformed on the morning of the second, in order that each might be by itself, and
to correct some things not done well during the hasty formations here the day before.

To the right of the First Corps, and on an extension of the
same line, along the crest and down the southeastern slope
of Culp's Hill, was posted the Twelfth Corps (General
Slocum) its right, which was the extreme right of the line of
the army, resting near a small stream called Rock Run. No
changes, that I am aware of, occurred in the formation of

this Corps, on the morning of the 2nd. The Second Corps, after the brief halt that I have mentioned, moved up and took position, its right resting upon the Taneytown Road, at the left of the Eleventh Corps, and extending the line thence, nearly a half mile, almost due south, towards Round Top, with its divisions in the following order, from right to left: The Third (General Alex Hays); the Second (Gibbon's; General Harrow temporarily); the First (General Caldwell). The formation was in line by brigade in column, the brigade being in column by regiment, with forty paces interval between regimental lines, the Second and Third Divisions having each one, and the First Division, two brigades—there were four brigades in the First—similarly formed, in reserve, 150 paces in the rear of the line of their respective divisions. That is, the line of the Corps, exclusive of its reserves, was the length of six regiments, deployed,[2] and the intervals between them, some of which were left wide for the posting of the batteries, and consisted of four common deployed lines, each of two ranks of men, and a little more than one-third over in reserve.

The five batteries, in all twenty-eight guns, were posted as follows: Woodruff's regular, six twelve-pound napoleons, brass, between the two brigades, in line of the Third Division; Arnold's "A" First Rhode Island, six three-inch parrotts, rifled, and Cushing's Regular, four three-inch Ordinance,

---

2. As the Second and Third Divisions had three brigades each, it follows that two brigades from each of the three divisions were in the front line.—ED.

rifled, between the Third and Second Division; Hazard's, (commanded during the battle by Lieutenant Brown,) "B" First Rhode Island, and Rhorty's N.G. each, six twelve-pound napoleons, brass, between the Second and First Division.

I have been thus specific in the description of the posting and formation of the Second Corps, because they were works that I assisted to perform; and also that the other Corps were similarly posted, with reference to the strength of the lines, and the intermixing of infantry and artillery. From this, you may get a notion of the whole.

The Third Corps (General Sickles) the remainder of it arriving upon the field this morning, was posted upon the left of the Second extending the line still in the direction of Round Top, with its left resting near Little Round Top. The left of the Third Corps was the extreme left of the line of battle, until changes occurred, which will be mentioned in the proper place. The Fifth Corps (General Sykes) coming on the Baltimore Pike about this time, was massed there, near the line of the battle, and held in reserve until sometime in the afternoon, when it changed position, as I shall describe.

I cannot give a detailed account of the cavalry, for I saw but little of it. It was posted near the wings, and watched the roads and the movements of the enemy upon the flanks of the enemy, but further than this participated but little in the battle. Some of it was also used for guarding the trains, which were far to the rear. The artillery reserve, which consisted of a good many batteries, were posted between the

Baltimore Pike and the Taneytown Road, on very nearly the center of a direct line passing through the extremities of the wings. Thus it could be readily sent to any part of the line. The Sixth Corps—General Sedgwick—did not arrive upon the field until some time in the afternoon, but it was now not very far away, and was coming up rapidly on the Baltimore Pike. No fears were entertained that "Uncle John," as his men call General Sedgwick, would not be in the right place at the right time.

These dispositions were all made early, I think before 8:00 in the morning. Skirmishers were posted well out all around the line, and all put in readiness for battle. The enemy did not yet demonstrate himself. With a look at the ground now, I think you may understand the movements of the battle. From Round Top, by the line of battle, round to the extreme right, I suppose is about three miles. From this same eminence to the Cemetery, extends a long ridge or hill—more resembling a great wave than a hill, however—with its crest, which was the line of battle, quite direct, between the points mentioned. To the west of this, that is towards the enemy, the ground falls away by a very gradual descent, across the Emmetsburg Road, and then rises again, forming another ridge, nearly parallel to the first, but inferior in altitude, and something over 1000 yards away. A belt of woods extends partly along this second ridge, and partly farther to the west, at distances of from 1000 to 1300 yards away from our line. Between these ridges, and along their slopes, that is, in front of the Second and Third Corps, the ground is cultivated, and is covered with fields of wheat, now nearly ripe, with grass and pastures, with some peach orchards, with fields of waving corn, and some farmhouses, and their out buildings along the Emmetsburg Road. There are very few places within the limits mentioned where troops and guns could move concealed. There are some oaks of considerable growth along the position of the right of the Second Corps, a group of small trees, sassafras and oak, in front of the right of the Second Division of this corps also; and considerable woods immediately in front of the left of the Third Corps, and also to the west of, and near Round Top. At the Cemetery, where is Cemetery Ridge, to which the line of the Eleventh Corps conforms, is the highest point in our line, except Round Top. From this the ground falls quite abruptly to the town, the nearest point of which is some 500 yards away from the line, and is cultivated, and checkered with stone fences.

The same is the character of the ground occupied by, and in front of the left of the First Corps, which is also on a part of Cemetery Ridge. The right of this Corps, and the whole of the Twelfth, are along Culp's Hill, and in woods, and the ground is very rocky, and in places in front precipitous—a most admirable position for defense from an attack in front, where, on account of the woods, no artillery could be used with effect by the enemy. Then these last three mentioned Corps, had, by taking rails, by appropriating stone fences, by felling trees, and digging the earth, during the night of the first of July, made for themselves excellent breastworks, which were a very good thing indeed. The position of the First and Twelfth Corps was admirably strong, therefore. Within the line of battle is an irregular basin, somewhat woody and rocky in places, but presenting few obstacles to the moving of troops and guns, from place to place along the lines, and also affording the advantage that all such movements, by reason of the surrounding crests, were out of view of the enemy. On the whole this was an admirable position to fight a defensive battle, good enough, I thought, when I saw it first, and better I believe than could be found elsewhere in a circle of many miles. Evils, sometimes at least, are blessings in disguise, for the repulse of our forces, and the death of Reynolds, on the first of July, with the opportune arrival of Hancock to arrest the tide of fugitives and fix it on these heights, gave us this position—perhaps the position gave us the victory. On arriving upon the field, General Meade established his headquarters at a shabby little farmhouse on the left of the Taneytown Road, the house nearest the line, and a little more than five hundred yards in the rear of what became the center of the position of the Second Corps, a point where he could communicate readily and rapidly with all parts of the army. The advantages of the position, briefly, were these: the flanks were quite well protected by the natural defenses there, Round Top up the left, and a rocky, steep, untraversable ground up the right. Our line was more elevated than that of the enemy, consequently our artillery had a greater range and power than theirs. On account of the convexity of our line, every part of the line

General Meade's headquarters

could be reinforced by troops having to move a shorter distance than if the line were straight; further, for the same reason, the line of the enemy must be concave, and, consequently, longer, and with an equal force, thinner, and so weaker than ours. Upon those parts of our line which were wooded, neither we nor the enemy could use artillery; but they were so strong by nature, aided by art, as to be readily defended by a small, against a very large, body of infantry. When the line was open, it had the advantage of having open country in front, consequently, the enemy here could not surprise, as we were on a crest, which besides the other advantages that I have mentioned, had this: the enemy must advance to the attack up an ascent, and must therefore move slower, and be, before coming upon us, longer under our fire, as well as more exhausted. These, and some other things, rendered our position admirable—for a defensive battle.

So, before a great battle, was ranged the Army of the Potomac. The day wore on, the weather still sultry, and the sky overcast, with a mizzling effort at rain. When the audience has all assembled, time seems long until the curtain rises; so today. "Will there be a battle today?" "Shall we attack the Rebel?" "Will he attack us?" These and similar questions, later in the morning, were thought or asked a million times.

Meanwhile, on our part, all was put in the last state of readiness for battle. Surgeons were busy riding about selecting eligible places for hospitals, and hunting streams, and springs, and wells. Ambulances, and ambulance men, were brought up near the lines, and stretchers gotten ready for use. Who of us could tell but that he would be the first to need them? The Provost Guards were busy driving up all stragglers, and causing them to join their regiments. Ammunition wagons were driven to suitable places, as were packed mules bearing boxes of cartridges; and the commands were informed where they might be found. Officers were sent to see that the men had each his hundred rounds of ammunition. Generals and their Staffs were riding here and there among their commands to see that all was right. A staff officer, or an orderly might be seen galloping furiously in the transmission of some order or message. All, all was ready and yet the sound of no gun had disturbed the air or ear today.

And so the men stacked their arms—in long bristling rows they stood along the crests—and were at ease. Some men of the Second and Third Corps pulled down the rail fences near and piled them up for breastworks in their front.

Some loitered, some went to sleep upon the ground, some, a single man, carrying twenty canteens slung over his shoulder, went for water. Some made them a fire and boiled a dipper of coffee. Some with knees cocked up, enjoyed the soldier's peculiar solace, a pipe of tobacco. Some were mirthful and chatty, and some were serious and silent. Leaving them thus—I suppose of all arms and grades there were about a hundred thousand of them somewhere about that field— each to pass the hour according to his duty or his humor, let us look to the enemy.

Here let me state, that according to the best information that I could get, I think a fair estimate of the Rebel force engaged in this battle would be a little upwards of a 100,000 men of all arms. Of course we can't now know, but there are reasonable data for this estimate. At all events there was no great disparity of numbers in the two opposing armies. We thought the enemy to be somewhat more numerous than we, and he probably was.[3] But if ninety-five men should fight with a hundred and five, the latter would not always be victors—and slight numerical differences are of much less consequence in great bodies of men.

---

3. The returns of the Union army for June 30 gave 89,238 infantry and artillery, and 14,973 cavalry "present for duty." If there is deducted 5,520 in three brigades of the Sixth Corps and 2,337 in detachments, which, although available, were not opposed to the enemy, and the usual percent of nomcombatants, 88,289 remains for the number engaged. The number engaged on the Confederate side in the same manner, is estimated at 75,000 from the returns of May 31, July 20 and July 31. See Livermore's *Numbers and Losses*, pp. 69, 102, 103.—ED.

Skillful generalship and good fighting are the jewels of war. These concurring are difficult to overcome; and these, not numbers, must determine this battle.

During all the morning — and of the night, too — the skirmishers of the enemy had been confronting those of the Eleventh, First, and Twelfth Corps. At the time of the fight of the First, he was seen in heavy force north of the town — he was believed to be now in the same neighborhood, in full force. But from the woody character of the country, and thereby the careful concealment of troops, which the Rebel is always sure to effect, during the early part of the morning almost nothing was actually seen by us of the invaders of the north. About 9:00 in the morning, I should think, our glasses began to reveal them at the west and northwest of the town, a mile and a half away from our lines. They were moving towards our left, but the woods of Seminary Ridge so concealed them that we could not make out much of their movements. About this time, some rifled guns in the Cemetery, at the left of the Eleventh Corps, opened fire — almost the first shots of any kind this morning — and when it was found they were firing at a Rebel line of skirmishers merely, that were advancing upon the left of that, and the right of the Second Corps, the officer in charge of the guns was ordered to cease firing, and was rebuked for having fired at all. These skirmishers soon engaged those at the right of the Second Corps, who stood their ground and were reinforced to make the line entirely secure. The Rebel skirmish line kept extending further and further to their right — toward our left. They would dash up close upon ours and sometimes drive them back a short distance, in turn to be repulsed themselves—and so they continued to do until their right was opposite the extreme left of the Third Corps. By these means they had ascertained the position and extent of our lines—but their own masses were still out of view. From the time that the firing commenced, as I have mentioned, it was kept up, among the skirmishers, until quite noon, often briskly; but with no definite results further than those mentioned, and with no considerable show of infantry on the part of the enemy to support. There was a farmhouse and outbuildings in front of the Third Division of the Second Corps at which the skirmishers of the enemy had made a dash, and dislodged ours posted there, and from there their sharp shooters began to annoy our line of skirmishers and even the main line, with their long-range rifles. I was up to the line, and a bullet from one of the rascals hid there, hissed by my cheek so close that I felt the movement of the air distinctly. And so I was not at all displeased when I saw one of our regiments go down and attack and capture the house and buildings and several prisoners, after a spirited little fight, and, by General Hays's order, burn the buildings to the ground. About noon the Signal Corps, from the top of Little Round Top, with their powerful glasses, and the cavalry at the extreme left, began to report the enemy in heavy force, making disposition of battle, to the west of Round Top, and opposite to the left of the Third Corps. Some few prisoners had been captured, some deserters from the enemy had come in, and from all sources, by this time, we had much important and reliable information of the enemy—of his disposition and apparent purposes. The Rebel infantry consisted of three Army Corps, each consisting of three divisions; Longstreet, Ewell—the same whose leg Gibbon's shell knocked off at Gainesville on the 28th of August last year—and A. P. Hill, each in the Rebel service having the rank of Lieutenant General, were the commanders of these Corps. Longstreet's division commanders were Hood, McLaws and Pickett; Ewell's were Rhodes, Early, and Johnson; and Hill's were Pender, Heth, and Anderson. Stewart and Fitzhugh Lee commanded divisions of the Rebel cavalry. The rank of these divisions commands, I believe, was that of Major General. The Rebels had about as much artillery as we did, but we never have thought much of this arm in the hands of our adversaries. They have courage enough, but not the skill to handle it well. They generally fire far too high, and the ammunition is usually of a very inferior quality. And, of late, we have begun to despise the enemy's cavalry too. It used to have enterprise and dash, but in the late cavalry contests ours have always been victorious, and so now we think about all this chivalry is fit for is to steal a few of our mules occasionally, and their negro drivers. This army of the rebel infantry, however, is good—to deny this is useless. I never had any desire to—and if one should count up, it would possibly be found that they have gained more victories over us, than we have over them, and they will now, doubtless, fight well, even desperately. And it is not horses or cannon that will determine the result of this confronting of the two armies, but the men with the muskets must do it— the infantry must do the sharp work. So we watched all this posting of forces as closely as possible, for it was a matter of vital interest to us, and all information relating to it was hurried to the commander of the army. The Rebel line of battle was concave, bending around our own, with extremities of the wings opposite to, or a little outside of ours. Longstreet's corps was upon their right; Hill's in the center. These two Rebel corps occupied the second or inferior ridge to the west of our position, as I have mentioned, with Hill's left bending towards, and resting near the town, and Ewell's was upon their left, his troops being in and to the east of the town. This last corps confronted our Twelfth, First, and the right of the Eleventh Corps. When I have said that ours was a good *defensive* position, this is equivalent to saying that that of the enemy was not a good *offensive* one; for these are relative terms, and cannot be both predicated of the respective positions of the two armies at the same time. The reasons that this was not a good offensive position, are the same already stated in favor of ours for defense. Excepting, occasionally, for a brief time, during some movement of troops, as when advancing to attack, their men and guns were kept constantly and carefully, by woods and inequalities of ground, out of our view.

Noon is past, 1:00 is past, and, we save the skirmishing that I have mentioned and an occasional shot from our guns, at something or other, the nature of which the ones who

fired it were ignorant, there was no fight yet. Our arms were
still stacked, and the men at ease. As I looked upon those
interminable rows of muskets along the crests, and saw how
cool and good spirited the men were, who were lounging
about on the ground among them, I could not, and did not,
have any fears as to the result of the battle. The storm was
near, and we all knew it well enough by this time, which was
to rain death upon these crests and down their slopes, and
yet the men who could not, and would not, escape it were as
calm and cheerful, generally, as if nothing unusual were
about to happen. You see, these men were veterans and had
been in such places so often that they were accustomed to
them. But I was well pleased with the tone of the men today—I could almost see the foreshadowing of victory upon
their faces, I thought. And I thought, too, as I had seen the
mighty preparations go on to completion for this great
conflict—the marshaling of these 200,000 men and the
guns of the hosts, that now but a narrow valley divided, that
to have been in such a battle, and to survive on the side of
the victors, would be glorious. Oh, the world is most
unchristian yet!

Somewhat after one 1:00 P.M.—the skirmish firing had
nearly ceased now—a movement of the Third Corps occurred, which I shall describe. I cannot conjecture the reason
for this movement. From the position of the Third Corps, as
I have mentioned, to the second ridge west, the distance is
about a thousand yards, and there the Emmetsburg Road
runs near the crest of the ridge. General Sickles commenced

to advance his whole corps, from the general line, straight to the front, with a view to occupy this second ridge along, and near the road. What his purpose could have been is past conjecture. It was not ordered by General Meade, as I heard him say, and he disapproved of it as soon as it was made known to him. Generals Hancock and Gibbon, as they saw the move in progress, criticized its propriety sharply, as I know, and foretold quite accurately what would be the result. I suppose the truth probably is that General Sickles supposed he was doing for the best; but he was neither born nor bred a soldier. But one can scarcely tell what may have been the motives of such a man—a politician, and some other things, exclusive of the Barton Key affair—a man after show and notoriety, and newspaper fame, and the adulation of the mob! Oh! There is a grave responsibility on those in whose hands are the lives of 10,000 men; and on those who put stars upon men's shoulders, too! Bah! I kindle when I see some things that I have to see. But this move of the Third Corps was an important one—it developed the battle—the results of the move to the corps itself we shall see. Oh! If this corps had kept its strong position upon the crest, and supported by the rest of the army, had waited for the attack of the enemy!

It was magnificent to see those 10,000 or 12,000 men[4]— they were good men — with their batteries, and some squadrons of cavalry upon the left flank, all in battle order,

4. The returns give 12,630 "present for duty" in the Third Corps. See 43 War Records, 151.—ED.

in several lines, with flags streaming, sweep steadily down the slope, across the valley, and up the next ascent, toward their destined position! From our position we could see it all. In advance Sickles pushed forward his heavy line of skirmishers, who drove back those of the enemy, across the Emmetsburg Road, and thus cleared the way for the main body. The Third Corps now became the absorbing object of interest of all eyes. The Second Corps took arms, and the first division of this corps was ordered to be in readiness to support the Third Corps, should circumstances render support necessary. As the Third Corps was the extreme left of our line, as it advanced, if the enemy was assembling to the west of Round Top with a view to turn our left, as we had heard, there would be nothing between the left flank of the Corps and the enemy, and the enemy would be square upon its flank by the time it had attained the road. So when this advance line came near the Emmetsburg Road, and we saw the squadrons of cavalry mentioned come dashing back from their position as flankers, and the smoke of some guns, and we heard the reports away to Sickles's left, anxiety became an element in our interest in these movements. The enemy opened slowly at first, and from long range; but he was square upon Sickles's left flank. General Caldwell was ordered at once to put his division—the First of the Second Corps, as mentioned—in motion, and to take post in the woods at the left slope of Round Top, in such a manner as to resist the enemy should he attempt to come around Sickles' left and gain his rear. The division moved as ordered, and disappeared from view in the woods, towards the point indicated at between 2:00 and 3:00 P.M., and the reserve brigade—the First, Colonel Heath temporarily commanding—of the Second Division, was therefore move up and occupied the position vacated by the Third Division. About the same time the Fifth Corps could be seen marching by the flank from its position on the Baltimore Pike, and in the opening of the woods heading for the same locality where the First Division of the Second Corps had gone. The Sixth Corps had now come up and was halted upon the Baltimore Pike. So the plot thickened. As the enemy opened upon Sickles with his batteries, some five or six in all, I suppose, firing slowly, Sickles with as many replied, and with much more spirit. The artillery fire became quite animated, soon; but the enemy was forced to withdraw his guns farther and farther away, and ours advanced upon him. It was not long before the cannonade ceased altogether, the enemy having retired out of range, and Sickles, having temporarily halted his command, pending this, moved forward again to the position he desired, or nearly that. It was now about 5:00, and we shall soon see what Sickles gained by his move. First we hear more artillery firing upon Sickles's left—the enemy seems to be opening again—and as we watch, the Rebel batteries seem to be advancing there. The cannonade is soon opened again, and with great spirit upon both sides. The enemy's batteries press those of Sickles, and pound the shot upon them, and this time they in turn begin to retire to position nearer the infantry. The enemy seems to be fearfully in earnest this time. And what is more ominous than the thunder or the shot of his advancing guns, this time, in the intervals between his batteries, far to Sickles's left, appear the long lines and the columns of the Rebel infantry, now unmistakably moving out to the attack. The position of the Third Corps becomes at once one of great peril, and it is probable that its commander by this time began to realize his true situation. All was astir now on our crest. Generals and their staffs were galloping hither and thither—the men were all in their places, and you might have heard the rattle of 10,000 ramrods as they drove home and "thugged" upon the little globes and cones of lead. As the enemy was advancing upon Sickles's flank, he commenced a change, or at least a partial one, of front, by swinging back his left and throwing forward his right, in order that his lines might be parallel to those of his adversary, his batteries meantime doing what they could to check the enemy's advance; but this movement was not completely executed before new Rebel batteries opened upon Sickles's right flank—his former front and in the same quarter appeared the Rebel infantry also. Now came the dreadful battle picture, of which we for a time could be but spectators. Upon the front and right flank of Sickles came sweeping the infantry of Longstreet and Hill. Hitherto there had been skirmishing and artillery practice—now the battle began; for amid the heavier smoke and larger tongues of flame of the batteries, now began to appear the countless flashes, and the long fiery sheets of the muskets, and the rattle of the volleys, mingled with the thunder of the guns. We see the long gray lines come sweeping down upon Sickles's front, and mix with the battle smoke; now the same colors emerge from the bushes and orchards upon his right, and envelope his flank in the confusion of the conflict.

Oh! The din and the roar, and these 30,000 Rebel wolf cries! What a hell is there down that valley! These ten or twelve thousand men of the Third Corps fight well, but it soon becomes apparent that they must be swept from the field, or perish there where they are doing so well, so thick and overwhelming a storm of Rebel fire involves them. It was fearful to see, but these men, such as ever escape, must come from that conflict as best they can. To move down and support them with other troops is out of the question, for this would be to do as Sickles did, to relinquish a good position, and advance to a bad one. There is no other alternative—the Third Corps must fight itself out of its position of destruction! What was it ever put there for?

In the meantime some other dispositions must be made to meet the enemy, in the event that Sickles is overpowered. With this corps out of the way, the enemy would be in a position to advance upon the line of the Second Corps, not in a line parallel with its front, but they would come obliquely from the left. To meet this contingency the left of the Second Division of the Second Corps is thrown back slightly, and two Regiments, the Fifteenth Massachusetts (Colonel Ward) and the Eighty-second New York (Lieutenant Colonel Horton), are advanced down to the Emmetsburg Road, to a favorable position nearer us than the fight has yet come, and some new batteries from the artillery reserve are posted upon the crest near the left of the Second Corps. This was all General Gibbon could do. Other dispositions were made or were now being made upon the field, which I shall mention presently. The enemy is still giving Sickles fierce battle—or rather the Third Corps, for Sickles has been borne from the field minus one of his legs, and General Birney now commands—and we of the Second Corps, a thousand yards away, with our guns and men are, and must be, still idle spectators of the fight.

The Rebel, as anticipated, tries to gain the left of the Third Corps, and for this purpose is now moving into the woods at the west of Round Top. We knew what he would find there. No sooner had the enemy gotten a considerable force into the woods mentioned, in the attempted execution of his purpose, than the roar of the conflict was heard there also. The Fifth Corps and the First Division of the Second were there at the right time, and promptly engaged him; and there, too, the battle soon became general and obstinate. Now the roar of battle has become twice the volume that it was before, and its range extends over more than twice the space. The Third Corps has been pressed back considerably, and the wounded are streaming to the rear by hundreds, but still the battle there goes on, with no considerable abatement on our part. The field of actual conflict extends now from a point to the front of the left of the Second Corps, away down to the front of Round Top, and the fight rages with the greatest fury. The fire of artillery and infantry and the yells of the Rebels fill the air with a mixture of hideous sounds. When the First Division of the Second Corps first engaged the enemy, for a time it was pressed back somewhat, but under the able and judicious management of General Caldwell, and the support of the Fifth Corps, it speedily ceased to retrograde, and stood its ground; and then there followed a time, after the Fifth Corps became well engaged, when from appearances we hoped the troops already engaged would be able to check entirely, or repulse the further assault of the enemy. But fresh bodies of the Rebels continued to advance out of the woods to the front of the position of the Third Corps, and to swell the numbers of the assailants of this already hard-pressed command. The men there begin to show signs of exhaustion—their ammunition must be nearly expended—they have now been fighting more than an hour, and against greatly superior numbers. From the sound of the firing at the extreme left, and the place where the smoke rises above the tree tops there, we know that the Fifth Corps is still steady, and holding its own there; and as we see the Sixth Corps now marching and near at hand to that point, we have no fears for the left—we have more apparent reason to fear for ourselves.

The Third Corps is being overpowered—here and there its lines begin to break—the men begin to pour back to the rear in confusion—the enemy are close upon them and among them—organization is lost to a great degree—guns and caissons are abandoned and in the hands of the enemy—the Third Corps, after a heroic but unfortunate fight, is being literally swept from the field. That corps gone, what is there between the Second Corps, and these yelling masses of the enemy? Do you not think that by this time we began to feel a personal interest in this fight? We did indeed. We had been mere observers—the time was at hand when we must be actors in this drama.

Up to this hour General Gibbon had been in command of the Second Corps, since yesterday, but General Hancock, relieved of his duties elsewhere, now assumed command. Five or six hundred yards away the Third Corps was making its last opposition; and the enemy was hotly pressing his advantages there, and throwing in fresh troops whose line extended still more along our front, when Generals Hancock and Gibbon rode along the lines of their troops; and at once cheer after cheer—not Rebel, mongrel cries, but genuine cheers—rang out all along the line, above the roar of battle, for "Hancock" and "Gibbon," and "our Generals." These were good. Had you heard their voices, you would have known these men would fight. Just at this time we saw another thing that made us glad: we looked to our rear, and there, and all up the hillside which was the rear of the Third Corps before it went forward, were rapidly advancing large bodies of men from the extreme right of our line of battle, coming to the support of the part now so hotly pressed. There was the whole Twelfth Corps, with the exception of about one brigade, that is, the larger portion of the divisions of Gens. Williams and Geary; the Third Division of the First

Corps, General Doubleday; and some other brigades from the same Corps—and some of them were moving at the double quick. They formed lines of battle at the foot of the Taneytown Road, and when the broken fragments of the Third Corps were swarming by them towards the rear, without halting or wavering they came sweeping up, and with glorious old cheers, under fire, took their places on the crest in line of battle to the left of the Second Corps. Now Sickles's blunder is repaired. Now, Rebel chief, hurl forward your howling lines and columns! Yell out your loudest and your last, for many of your best will never yell, or wave the spurious flag again!

The battle still rages all along the left, where the Fifth Corps is, and the west slope of Round Top is the scene of the conflict; and nearer us there was but short abatement, as the last of the Third Corps retired from the field, for the enemy is flushed with his success. He has been throwing forward brigade after brigade, and division after division, since the battle began, and his advancing line now extends almost as far to our right as the right of the Second Division of the Second Corps. The whole slope in our front is full of them; and in various formation, in line, in column, and in masses which are neither, with yells and thick volleys, they are rushing towards our crest. The Third Corps is out of the way. Now we are in for it. The battery men are ready by their loaded guns. All along the crest is ready. Now Arnold and Brown; now Cushing, and Woodruff, and Rhorty!—you three shall survive today! They drew the cords that moved the friction primers, and gun after gun, along the batteries, in rapid succession, leaped where it stood and bellowed its canister upon the enemy. The enemy still advance. The infantry open fire; first the two advance regiments, the Fifteenth Massachusetts and the Eighty-second New York, then here and there throughout the length of the long line, at the points where the enemy comes nearest, and soon the whole crest, artillery and infantry, is one continued sheet of fire. From Round Top to near the Cemetery stretches an uninterrupted field of conflict. There is a great army upon each side, now hotly engaged.

To see the fight, while it went on in the valley below us, was terrible—what must it be now, when we are in it, and it is all around us, in all its fury?

All senses for the time are dead but the one of sight. The roar of the discharges and the yells of the enemy all pass unheeded; but the impassioned soul is all eyes, and sees all things, that the smoke does not hide. How madly the battery men are driving home the double charges of canister in those broad-mouthed napoleons, whose fire seems almost to reach the enemy. How rapidly these long, blue-coated lines of infantry deliver their file fire down the slope.

But there is no faltering—the men stand nobly to their work. Men are dropping dead or wounded on all sides, by scores and by hundreds, and the poor mutilated creatures, some with an arm dangling, some with a leg broken by a bullet, are limping and crawling towards the rear. They make no sound of complaint or pain, but are as silent as if dumb and mute. A sublime heroism seems to pervade all, and the intuition that to lose that crest, all is lost. How our officers, in the work of cheering on and directing the men, are falling.

We have heard that General Zook and Colonel Cross, in the First Division of our corps, are mortally wounded — they both commanded brigades — now near us Colonel Ward of the Fifteenth Massachusetts — he lost a leg at Balls Bluff — and Lieutenant Colonel Horton of the Eighty-second New York, are mortally struck while trying to hold their commands, which are being forced back; Colonel Revere, Twentieth Massachusetts, grandson of old Paul Revere of the Revolution, is killed; Lieutenant Colonel Max Thoman, commanding Fifty-ninth New York, is mortally wounded; and a host of others that I cannot name. These were of Gibbon's division. Lieutenant Brown is wounded among his guns — his position is a hundred yards in advance of the main line — the enemy is upon his battery, and he escapes, but leaves three of his six guns in the hands of the enemy.

The fire all along our crest is terrific, and it is a wonder how anything human could have stood before it, and yet the madness of the enemy drove them on, clear up to the muzzle of the guns, clear up to the lines of our infantry — but the lines stood right in their places. General Hancock and his aides rode up to Gibbon's division, under the smoke. General Gibbon, with myself, was near, and there was a flag dimly visible, coming towards us from the direction of the enemy. "Here, what are these men falling back for?" said

Hancock. The flag was no more than fifty yards away, but it was the head of a Rebel column, which at once opened fire with a volley. Lieutenant Miller, General Hancock's aide, fell, twice struck, but the General was unharmed, and he told the First Minnesota, which was near, to drive these people away. That splendid regiment, the less than 300 that are left out of 1500 that it has had, swings around upon the enemy, gives them a volley in their faces, and advances upon them with the bayonet. The Rebels fled in confusion, but Colonel Colville, Lieutenant Colonel Adams, and Major Downie are all badly, dangerously wounded, and many of the other officers and men will never fight again. More than two-thirds fell.

Such fighting as this cannot last long. It is now near sundown, and the battle has gone on wonderfully long already. But if you will stop to notice it, a change has occurred. The Rebel cry has ceased, and the men of the Union begin to shout there, under the smoke, and their lines to advance. See, the Rebels are breaking! They are in confusion in all our front! The wave has rolled upon the rock, and the rock has smashed it. Let us shout, too!

First upon their extreme left the Rebels broke, where they had almost pierced our lines; thence the repulse extended rapidly to their right. They hung longest about Round Top, where the Fifth Corps punished them, but in a space of time incredibly short, after they first gave signs of weakness, the whole force of the Rebel assault along the whole line—in spite of waving red flags, and yells, and the entreaties of

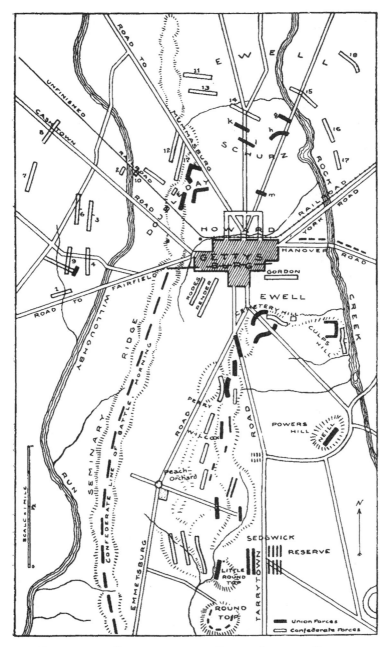

BATTLE OF GETTYSBURG — FINAL ATTACK, JULY 2
Compiled by C.E. Estabrook

officers, and the pride of the chivalry—fled like chaff before the whirlwind, back down the slope, over the valley, across the Emmetsburg Road, shattered, without organization in utter confusion, fugitive into the woods, and victory was with the arms of the Republic. The great Rebel assault, the greatest ever made upon this continent, has been made and signally repulsed, and upon this part of the field the fight of today is now soon over. Pursuit was made as rapidly and as far as practicable, but owing to the proximity of night, and the long distance which would have to be gone over before any of the enemy, where they would be likely to halt, could be overtaken, further success was not attainable today. Where the Rebel rout first commenced, a large number of prisoners, some thousands at least, were captured; almost all their dead, and such of their wounded as could not themselves get to the rear, were within our lines; several of their flags were gathered up, and a good many thousand muskets, some nine or ten guns and some caissons lost by the Third Corps, and the three of Brown's battery—these last were in Rebel hands but a few minutes—were all safe now with us, the enemy having had no time to take them off.

Not less, I estimate, than 20,000 men were killed or wounded in this fight. Our own losses must have been nearly half this number—about 4,000 in the Third Corps, fully 2,000 in the Second, and I think 2,000 in the Fifth, and I think the losses of the First, Twelfth, and a little more than a brigade of the Sixth—all of that corps which was actually engaged—would reach nearly 2,000 more.[5] Of course it will never be possible to know the numbers upon either side who fell in this particular part of the general battle, but from the position of the enemy and his numbers, and the appearance of the field, his loss must have been as heavy, or as I think much heavier than our own, and my estimates are probably short of the actual loss.

The fight done, the sudden revulsions of sense and feeling follow, which more or less characterize all similar occasions. How strange the stillness seems! The whole air roared with the conflict but a moment since—now all is silent; not a gunshot sound is heard, and the silence comes distinctly, almost painfully to the senses. And the sun purples the clouds in the west, and the sultry evening steals on as if there had been no battle, and the furious shout and the cannon's roar had never shaken the earth. And how look these fields? We may see them before dark—the ripening grain, the luxuriant corn, the orchards, the grassy meadows, and in their midst the rural cottage of brick or wood. They were beautiful this morning. They are desolate now—trampled by the countless feet of the combatants, plowed and scored by the shot and shell, the orchards splintered, the fences prostrate, the harvest trodden in the mud. And more dreadful than the sight of all this, thickly strewn over all their length and

---

5. The returns give the total loss in the battle as follows: 1,275 in First Division of Second Corps; 4,211 in Third Corps; 2,187 in Fifth Corps; 242 in Sixth Corps. Substantially all these losses were suffered July 2. See 43 War Records. The losses in the First Corps and Second Division of Second Corps on July 2 cannot be separated from those of July 1 and 3 in the War Records.—ED.

breadth, are the habiliments of the soldiers, the knapsacks cast aside in the stress of the fight, or after the fatal lead had struck; haversacks, yawning with the rations the owner will never call for; canteens of cedar of the Rebel men of Jackson, and of cloth-covered tin of the men of the Union; blankets and trousers, and coats, and caps, and some are blue and some are gray; muskets and ramrods, and bayonets, and swords, and scabbards and belts, some bent and cut by the shot or shell; broken wheels, exploded caissons, and limber-boxes, and dismantled guns, and all these are sprinkled with blood; horses, some dead, a mangled heap of carnage, some alive, with a leg shot clear off, or other frightful wounds, appealing to you with almost more than brute gaze as you pass; and last, but not least numerous, many thousands of men—and there was no rebellion here now—the men of South Carolina were quiet by the side of those of Massachusetts, some composed, with upturned faces, sleeping the last sleep, some mutilated and frightful, some wretched, fallen, bathed in blood, survivors still and unwilling witnesses of the rage of Gettysburg.

And yet with all this before them, as darkness came on, and the dispositions were made and the outposts thrown out for the night, the Army of the Potomac was quite mad with joy. No more light-hearted guests ever graced a banquet than were these men as they boiled their coffee and munched their soldiers' supper tonight. Is it strange?

Otherwise they would not have been soldiers. And such sights as all these will be certain to be seen as long as war lasts in the world, and when war is done, then is the end, and the days of the millenium are at hand.

The ambulances commenced their work as soon as the battle opened—the twinkling lanterns through the night, and the sun of tomorrow saw them still with the same work unfinished.

I wish that I could write, that with the coming on of darkness, ended the fight of today, but such was not the case. The armies have fought enough today and ought to sleep tonight, one would think, but not so thought the Rebel. Let us see what he gained by his opinion. When the troops, including those of the Twelfth Corps had been withdrawn from the extreme right of our line, in the afternoon, to support the left, as I have mentioned, thereby, of course, weakening that part of the line so left, the Rebel Ewell, either becoming aware of the fact, or because he thought he could carry our right at all events, late in the afternoon commenced an assault upon that part of our line. His battle had been going on there simultaneously with the fight on the left, but not with any great degree of obstinacy on his part. He had advanced his men cautiously through the woods and in front of the formidable position lately held by the Twelfth Corps, and to his surprise, I have no doubt, found our strong defenses upon the extreme right, entirely abandoned. These he at once took possession of and simultaneously made an attack upon our right flank, which was now near the summit of Culp's Hill, and upon the front of that part of the line. That small portion of the Twelfth Corps, which had been left there, and some of the Eleventh Corps, sent to their assistance, did what they could to check the Rebels; but the Eleventh Corps men were getting shot at there, and they did not want to stay. Matters began to have a bad look in that part of the field. A portion of the First Division of the First Corps, was sent there for support — the Sixth Wisconsin, among others, and this improved matters — but still, as we had but a small number of men there, all told, the enemy with their great numbers, were having too much prospect of success, and it seems that, probably emboldened by this, Ewell had resolved upon a night attack upon that wing of the army, and was making his dispositions accordingly. The enemy had not at sundown, actually carried any part of our rifle pits there, save the ones abandoned, but he was getting troops assembled upon our flank, and altogether, with our weakness there, at that time, matters did not look as we would like to have them. Such was then the posture of affairs, when the fight upon our left, that I have described, was done. Under such circumstances it is not strange that the Twelfth Corps, as soon as its work was done upon the left, was quickly ordered back to the right, to its old position. There it arrived in good time; not soon enough, of course, to avoid the mortification of finding the enemy in the possession of a part of the works the men had labored so hard to construct, but in ample time before dark to put the men well in the pits we already held, and to take up a strong defensible position, at right angles to, and in rear of the main line, in order to resist these flanking dispositions of the enemy. The army was secure again. The men in the works would be steady against all attacks in front, as long as they knew that their flank was safe. Until between 10:00 and 11:00 at night, the woods upon the right resounded with the discharges of musketry. Shortly after or about dark, the enemy made a dash upon the right of the Eleventh Corps. They crept up the windings of a valley, not in a very heavy force, but from the peculiar mode in which this Corps does outpost duty, quite unperceived in the dark until they were close upon the main line. It is said, I do not know it to be true, that they spiked two guns of one of the Eleventh Corps' batteries, and that the battery men had to drive them off with their sabres and rammers, and that there was some fearful "Dutch" swearing on the occasion, *donner wetter* among other similar impious oaths, having been freely used. The enemy here were finally repulsed by the assistance of Colonel Correll's brigade of the Third Division of the Second Corps, and the Hundred-and-sixth Pennsylvania, from the Second Division of the same corps, was by General Howard's request sent there to do outpost duty. It seems to have been a matter of utter madness and folly on the part of the enemy to have continued their night attack, as they did upon the right. Our men were securely covered by ample works and even in most places, a log was placed a few inches above the top of the main breastwork, as a protection to the heads of the men as they thrust out their pieces beneath it to fire. Yet in the darkness, the enemy would rush up, clambering over rocks and among trees, even to the front of the works, but only to leave their riddled bodies there upon the ground or to be swiftly repulsed headlong into the woods again. In the darkness, the enemy would climb trees close to the works and endeavor to shoot our men by the light of the flashes. When discovered, a thousand bullets would whistle after them in the dark, and some would hit, and then the Rebel would make up his mind to come down.

Our loss was light, almost nothing in this fight—the next morning the enemy's dead were thick all along this part of the line. Near 11:00 the enemy, wearied with his disastrous work, desisted, and thereafter until morning, not a shot was heard in all the armies.

So much for the battle. There is another thing that I wish to mention, of the matters of the 2nd of July.

After evening came on, and from reports received, all was known to be going satisfactorily upon the right, General Meade summoned his corps commanders to his headquarters for consultation. A consultation is held upon matters of vast moment to the country, and that poor little farmhouse is honored with more distinguished guests than it ever had before, or than it will ever have again, probably.

Do you expect to see a degree of ceremony and severe military aspect characterize this meeting, in accordance with strict military rules and commensurate with the moment of the matters of their deliberation? Name it "Mayor General Meade, Commander of the Army of the Potomac, with his Corps Generals, holding a Council of War, upon the field of Gettysburg," and it would sound pretty well—

and that was what it was; and you might make a picture of it and hang it up by the side of *Napoleon and his Marshals* and *Washington and his Generals* maybe, at some future time. But for the artist to draw his picture from, I will tell how this council appeared. Meade, Sedgwick, Slocum, Howard, Hancock, Sykes, Newton, Pleasanton—commander of the cavalry—and Gibbon, were the generals present. Hancock, now that Sickles is wounded, has charge of the Third Corps, and Gibbon again has the Second. Meade is a tall, spare man, with full beard, which with his hair, originally brown, is quite thickly sprinkled with gray. He has a Romanish face, very large nose, and a white, large forehead—prominent and wide over the eyes, which are full and large, and quick in their movements—and he wears spectacles. His *fibers* are all of the long and sinewy kind. His habitual personal appearance is quite careless, and it would be rather difficult to make him look well dressed. Sedgwick is quite a heavy man, short, thickset and muscular, with florid complexion, dark, calm, straight-looking eyes, with full, heavyish features, which, with his eyes, have plenty of animation when he is aroused. He has a magnificent profile, well cut, with the nose and forehead forming almost a straight line, curly, short, chestnut hair and full beard, cut short, with a little gray in it. He dresses carelessly, but can look magnificently when he is well dressed. Like Meade, he looks—and is—honest and modest. You might see at once, why his men, because they love him, call him "Uncle John," not to his face, of course, but among themselves. Slocum is small, rather spare, with black, straight hair and beard, which latter is unshaven and thin, large, full, quick, black eyes, white skin, sharp nose, wide cheek bones, and hollow cheeks and small chin. His movements are quick and angular, and he dresses with a sufficient degree of elegance. Howard is medium in size, has nothing marked about him, is the youngest of them all—I think—has lost an arm in the war, has straight brown hair and beard, shaves his short upper lip, over which his nose slants down, dim blue eyes, and on the whole, appears a very pleasant, affable, well-dressed little gentleman. Hancock is the tallest and most shapely, and in many respects is the best-looking officer of them all. His hair is very light brown, straight and moist, and always looks well, his beard is of the same color, of which he wears the moustache and a tuft upon the chin; complexion ruddy, features neither large nor small, but well cut, with full jaw and chin, compressed mouth, straight nose, full, deep blue eyes, and a very mobile, emotional countenance. He always dresses remarkably well, and his manner is dignified, gentlemanly, and commanding. I think if he were in citizens' clothes, and should give commands in the army to those who did not know him, he would be likely to be obeyed at once, and without any question as to his right to command. Sykes is a small, rather thin man, well dressed and gentlemanly, brown hair and beard, which he wears full, with red, pinched, rough-looking skin, feeble blue eyes, long nose, and with the general air of one who is weary and a little ill-natured. Newton is a well-sized, shapely, muscular, well-dressed man, with brown hair, a very ruddy, clean-shaved, full face, blue eyes, blunt, round features, walks very erect, curbs in his chin, and has somewhat of that smart sort of swagger that people are apt to suppose characterizes soldiers. Pleasonton is quite a nice little dandy, with brown hair and beard, a straw hat with a little jockey rim, which he cocks upon one side of his head, with an unsteady eye, that looks slyly at you and then dodges. Gibbon, the youngest of them all, save Howard, is about the same size as Slocum, Howard, Sykes and Pleasanton, and there are none of these who will weigh 150 pounds. He is compactly made, neither spare nor corpulent, with ruddy complexion, chestnut brown hair, a clean-shaved face, except his moustache, which is decidedly reddish in color, medium-sized, well-shaped head, sharp, moderately jutting brow, deep blue, calm eyes, sharp, slightly acquiline nose, compressed mouth, full jaws and chin, with an air of calm firmness in his manner. He always looks well dressed. I suppose Howard is about thirty-five and Meade about forty-five years of age; the rest are between these ages, but not many under forty. As they come to the council now, there is the appearance of fatigue about them, which is not customary, but is only due to the hard labors of the past few days. They all wear clothes of dark blue, some have top boots and some not, and except the two-starred straps upon the shoulders of all save Gibbon, who has but one star, there was scarcely a piece of regulation uniform about them all. They wore their swords, of various patterns, but no sashes, the army hat, but with the crown pinched into all sorts of shapes and the rim slouched down and shorn of all its ornaments but the gilt band—except Sykes who wore a blue cap, and Pleasanton with his straw hat with broad black band. Then the mean little room where they met—its only furniture consisted of a large, wide bed in one corner, a small pine table in the center, upon which was a wooden pail of water, with a tin cup for drinking, and a candle, stuck to the table by putting the end in tallow melted down from the wick, and five or six straight-backed rush-bottomed chairs. The generals came in—some sat, some kept walking or standing, two lounged upon the bed, some were constantly smoking cigars. And thus disposed, they deliberated whether the army should fall back from its present position to one in rear which it was said was stronger, should attack the enemy on the morrow, wherever he could be found, or should stand there upon the horseshoe crest, still on the defensive, and await the further movements of the enemy.

The latter proposition was unanimously agreed to. Their heads were sound. The Army of the Potomac would just halt right there and allow the Rebel to come up and smash his head against it, to any reasonable extent he desired, as he had today. After some two hours the council dissolved, and the officers went their several ways.

Night, sultry and starless, droned on, and it was almost midnight that I found myself peering my way from the line of the Second Corps, back down to the General's headquarters, behind which was an ambulance, in a little peach orchard. All was silent now but for the sound of the ambu-lances, as they were bringing off the wounded, and you could hear them rattle here and there about the field, and see their lanterns. I am weary and sleepy, almost to such an extent as not to be able to sit on my horse. And my horse can hardly move—the spur will not start him—what can be the reason? I know that he has been touched by two or three bullets today, but not to wound or lame him to speak of. Then, in riding by a horse that is hitched, in the dark, I got kicked; had I not a very thick boot, the blow would have been likely to have broken my ankle—it did break my tem-per as it was—and, as if it would cure matters, I foolishly spurred my horse again. No use, he would but walk. I dis-mounted; I could not lead him along at all, so out of temper, I rode at the slowest possible walk to the headquarters, which I reached at last. Generals Hancock and Gibbon were asleep in the ambulance. With a light I found what was the matter with "Billy." A bullet had entered his chest just in front of my left leg, as I was mounted, and the blood was running down all his side and leg, and the air from his lungs came out of the bullet hole. I begged his pardon mentally for my cruelty in spurring him, and should have done so in words if he could have understood me. Kind treatment as is due to the wounded he could understand and he had it. Poor Billy! He and I were first under fire together, and I rode him at the second Bull Run and the first and second Fredericks-burg, and at Antietam after brave "Joe" was killed; but I shall never mount him again—Billy's battles are over.

"George, make my bed here upon the ground by the side of this ambulance. Pull off my sabre and my boots—that will do!" Was ever princely couch or softest down so soft as those rough blankets, there upon the unroofed sod? At midnight they received me for four hours delicious dreamless oblivion of weariness and of battle. So to me, ended the 2nd of July.

* * * * *

At 4:00 on the morning of the 3rd, I was awakened by General Gibbon's pulling me by the foot and saying: "Come, don't you hear that?" I sprang up to my feet. Where was I? A moment and my dead senses and memory were alive again, and the sound of brisk firing of musketry to the front and right of the Second Corps, and over at the extreme right of our line, where we heard it last in the night, brought all back to my memory. We surely were on the field of battle, and there were palpable evidences to my reason that today was to be another of blood. Oh! for a moment the thought of it was sickening to every sense and feeling! But the motion of my horse as I galloped over the crest a few minutes later, and the serene splendor of the morning now breaking through rifted clouds and spreading over the landscape soon reassured me. Come day of battle! Up Rebel hosts, and thunder with your arms! We are all ready to do and to die for the Republic!

I found a sharp skirmish going on in front of the right of the Second Corps, between our outposts and those of the enemy, but save this—and none of the enemy but his outposts were in sight—all was quiet in that part of the field. On the extreme right of the line the sound of musketry was quite heavy; and this I learned was brought on by the attack of the Second Division, Twelfth Corps (General Geary), upon the enemy in order to drive him out of our works which he had sneaked into yesterday, as I have mentioned. The attack was made at the earliest moment in the morning when it was light enough to discern objects to fire at. The enemy could not use the works, but was confronting Geary in woods, and had the cover of many rocks and trees, so the fight was an irregular one, now breaking out and swelling to a vigorous fight, now subsiding to a few scattering shots; and so it continued by turns until the morning was well advanced, when the enemy was finally wholly repulsed and driven from the pits, and the right of our line was again reestablished in the place it first occupied. The heaviest losses the Twelfth Corps sustained in all the battle, occurred during this attack, and they were here quite severe. I heard General Meade express dissatisfaction at General Geary for making this attack, as a thing not ordered and not necessary, as the works of ours were of no intrinsic importance, and had not been captured from us by a fight, and Geary's position was just as good as they, where he was during the night. And I heard General Meade say that he sent an order to have the fight stopped; but I believe the order was not communicated to Geary until after the repulse of the enemy. Late in the forenoon the enemy again tried to carry our right by storm. We heard that old Rebel Ewell had sworn an oath that he would break our right. He had Stonewall Jackson's corps, and possibly imagined himself another Stonewall, but he certainly *hankered* after the right of our line—and so up through the woods, and over the rocks, and up the steeps he sent his storming parties—our men could see them now in the daytime. But all the Rebel's efforts were fruitless, save in one thing, slaughter to his own men. These assaults were made with great spirit and determination, but as the enemy would come up, our men lying behind their secure defenses would just singe them with the blaze of their muskets, and riddle them, as a hailstorm the tender blades of corn. The Rebel oath was not kept any more than his former one to support the Constitution of the United States. The Rebel loss was very heavy indeed, here, ours but trifling. I regret that I cannot give more of the details of this fighting upon the right—it was so determined upon the part of the enemy, both last night and this morning—so successful to us. About all that I actually saw of it during its progress, was the smoke, and I heard the discharges. My information is derived from officers who were personally in it. Some of our heavier artillery assisted our infantry in this by firing, with the piece elevated, far from the rear, over the heads of our men, at a distance from the enemy of two miles, I suppose. Of course, they could have done no great damage. It was nearly 11:00 that the battle in this part of the field subsided, not to be again renewed. All the morning we felt no apprehension for this part of the line, for we knew its strength, and that our troops engaged, the Twelfth Corps and the

First Division, Wadsworth's, of the First, could be trusted.

For the sake of telling one thing at a time, I have anticipated events somewhat, in writing of this fight upon the right. I shall now go back to the starting point, 4:00 this morning, and, as other events occurred during the day, second to none in the battle in importance, which I think I saw as much of as any man living, I will tell you something of them, and what I saw, and how the time moved on. The outpost skirmish that I have mentioned, soon subsided. I suppose it was the natural escape of the wrath which the men had, during the night, hoarded up against each other, and which, as soon as they could see in the morning, they could no longer contain, but must let it off through their musket barrels, at their adversaries. At the commencement of the war such firing would have awaked the whole army and roused it to its feet and to arms; not so now. The men upon the crest lay snoring in their blankets, even though some of the enemy's bullet dropped among them, as if bullets were as harmless as the drops of dew around them. As the sun arose today, the clouds became broken, and we had once more glimpses of sky, and fits of sunshine—a rarity—to cheer us. From the crest, save to the right of the Second Corps, no enemy, not even his outposts, could be discovered along all the position where he so thronged upon the Third Corps yesterday. All was silent there—the wounded horses were limping about the field; the ravages of the conflict were still fearfully visible—the scattered arms and the ground thickly dotted with the dead—but no hostile foe. The men were roused early, in order that the morning meal might be out of the way in time for whatever should occur. Then ensued the hum of an army, not in ranks, chatting in low tones, and running about and jostling among each other, rolling and packing their blankets and tents. They looked like an army of rag-gatherers, while shaking these very useful articles of the soldier's outfit, for you must know that rain and mud in conjunction have not had the effect to make them clean, and the wear and tear of service have not left them entirely whole. But one could not have told by the appearance of the men, that they were in battle yesterday, and were likely to be again today. They packed their knapsacks, boiled their coffee, and munched their hard bread just as usual—just like old soldiers who know what campaigning is; and their talk is far more concerning their present employment—some joke or drollery—than concerning what they saw or did yesterday.

As early as practicable, the lines all along the left are revised and reformed, this having been rendered necessary by yesterday's battle and also by what is anticipated today.

It is the opinion of many of our Generals that the Rebel will not give us battle today—that he had enough yesterday—that he will be heading towards the Potomac at the earliest practicable moment, if he has not already done so; but the better, and controlling judgment is, that he will make another grand effort to pierce or turn our lines—that he will either mass and attack the left again, as yesterday, or direct his operations against the left of our center, the posi-

tion of the Second Corps, and try to sever our line. I infer
that General Meade was of the opinion that the attack today
would be upon the left—this from the disposition he ordered, I know that General Hancock anticipated the attack
upon the center.

The dispositions today upon the left are as follows:

The Second and Third Divisions of the Second Corps are
in the position of yesterday; then on the left come Doubleday's—the Third Division and Colonel Stannard's brigade
of the First Corps; then Colwell's—the First Division of the
Second Corps; then the Third Corps, temporarily under the
command of Hancock since Sickles's wound. The Third
Corps is upon the same ground in part, and on the identical
line where it first formed yesterday morning, and where, had
it stayed instead of moving out to the front, we should have
many more men today, and should not have been upon the
brink of disaster yesterday. On the left of the Third Corps is
the Fifth Corps, with a short front and deep line; then comes
the Sixth Corps, all but one brigade, which is sent over to
the Twelfth. The Sixth, splendid corps, almost intact in the
fight of yesterday, is the extreme left of our line, which,
terminates to the south of Round Top, and runs along its
western base, in the woods, and thence to the Cemetery.
This corps is burning to pay off the old scores made on the
4th of May, there back of Fredericksburg. Note well the
position of the Second and Third Divisions of the Second
Corps—it will become important. There are nearly 6,000
men and officers in these two divisions here upon the field—

the losses were quite heavy yesterday, some regiments are detached to other parts of the field—so all told there are less than 6,000 men now in the two divisions,[6] who occupy a line of about a thousand yards. The most of the way along this line upon the crest was a stone fence, constructed of small rough stones, a good deal of the way badly pulled down, but the men had improved it and patched it with rails from the neighboring fences, and with earth, so as to render it in many places a very passable breastwork against musketry and flying fragments of shells.

These works are so low as to compel the men to kneel or lie down generally to obtain cover. Near the right of the Second Division, and just by the little group of trees that I have mentioned there, this stone fence made a right angle, and extended thence to the front, about twenty or thirty yards, where with another less than a right angle it followed along the crest again.

The lines were conformed to these breastworks and to the nature of the ground upon the crest, so as to occupy the most favorable places, to be covered, and still be able to deliver effective fire upon the enemy should he come there. In some places a second line was so posted as to be able to deliver its fire over the heads of the first line behind the works; but such formation was not practicable all of the way. But all the force of these two divisions was in line, in

---

6. The returns of June 30 gave 7,546 "present for duty" in these two divisions, but five of their twenty-six regiments were not in this part of the battle. See 43 War Records, 53, 176–7, 435, 457, 462, 471.—ED.

position, without reserves, and in such a manner that every man of them could have fired his piece at the same instant. The division flags, that of the Second Division, being a white trefoil upon a square blue field, and of the Third Division, a blue trefoil upon a white rectangular field, waved behind the divisions at the points where the generals of division were supposed to be; the brigade flags, similar to these but with a triangular field, were behind the brigades; and the national flags of the regiments were in the lines of their regiments. To the left of the Second division, and advanced something over a hundred yards, were posted a part of Stannard's brigade— two regiments or more—behind a small bush-crowned crest that ran in a direction oblique to the general line. These were well covered by the crest, and wholly concealed by the bushes, so that an advancing enemy would be close upon them before they could be seen. Other troops of Doubleday's division were strongly posted in rear of these in the general line.

I could not help wishing all the morning that this line of the two divisions of the Second Corps was stronger; it was, so far as numbers constitute strength, the weakest part of our whole line of battle. What if, I thought, the enemy should make an assault here today with two or three heavy lines—a great overwhelming mass; would he not sweep through that thin 6,000?

But I was not General Meade, who alone had power to send other troops there; and he was satisfied with that part of the line as it was. He was early on horseback this morning, and rode along the whole line, looking to it himself, and with glass in hand sweeping the woods and fields in the direction of the enemy, to see if aught of him could be discovered. His manner was calm and serious, but earnest. There was no arrogance of hope, or timidity of fear discernible in his face; but you would have supposed he would do his duty conscientiously and well, and would be willing to abide the result. You would have seen this in his face. He was well pleased with the left of the line today, it was so strong with good troops. He had no apprehension for the right where the fight now was going on, on account of the admirable position of our forces there. He was not of the opinion that the enemy would attack the center, our artillery had such sweep there, and this was not the favorite point of attack with the Rebel. Besides, should he attack the center, the general thought he could reinforce it in good season. I heard General Meade speak of these matters to Hancock and some others, at about 9:00 in the morning, while they were up by the line, near the Second Corps.

No further changes of importance, except those mentioned, were made in the disposition of the troops this morning, except to replace some of the batteries that were disabled yesterday by others from the artillery reserve and to brace up the lines well with guns from the same source wherever there were eligible places. The line is all in good order again, and we are ready for general battle.

Save the operations upon the right, the enemy so far as we could see, was very quiet all the morning. Occasionally, the outposts would fire a battle and then cease. Movements would be discovered which would indicate the attempt on the part of the enemy to post a battery. Our parrotts would send a few shells to the spot, then silence would follow.

At one of these times a painful accident happened to us, this morning. First Lieutenant Henry Ropes, Twentieth Massachusetts, in General Gibbon's division, a most estimable gentleman and officer — intelligent, educated, refined, one of the noble souls that came to the country's defense—while lying at his post with his regiments, in front of one of the batteries, which fired over the infantry, was instantly killed by a badly made shell, which, or some portion of it, fell but a few yards in front of the muzzle of the gun. The same accident killed or wounded several others. The loss of Ropes would have pained us at any time, and in any manner; in this manner his death was doubly painful.

Between ten and 11:00, over in a peach orchard in front of the position of Sickles yesterday, some little show of the enemy's infantry was discovered; a few shells scattered the gray-backs; they again appeared, and it becoming apparent that they were only posting a skirmish line, no further molestation was offered them. A little after this, some of the enemy's flags could be discerned over near the same quarter, above the top and behind a small crest of a ridge. There seems to be two or three of them—possibly they were guidons—and they moved too fast to be carried on foot. Possibly, we thought, the enemy is posting some batteries there. We knew in about two hours from this time better about the matter. Eleven o'clock came. The noise of battle has ceased upon the right, not a sound of a gun or musket can be heard on all the field; the sky is bright, with only the white fleecy clouds floating over from the west. The July sun streams down its fire upon the bright iron of the muskets in stacks upon the crest, and the dazzling brass of the napoleons. The army lolls and longs for the shade, of which some get a hand's breadth, from a shelter tent stuck upon a ramrod. The silence and sultriness of a July noon are supreme. Now it so happened, that just about this time of day a very original and interesting thought occurred to General Gibbon and several of his staff; that it would be a very good thing, and a very good time, to have something to eat. When I announce to you that I had not tasted a mouthful of food since yesterday noon, and that all I had had to drink since that time, but the most miserable muddy warm water, was a little drink of whisky that Major Biddlep, General Meade's aide-de-camp, gave me last evening, and a cup of strong coffee that I gulped down as I was first mounting this morning, and further, that, save the four or five hours in the night, there was scarcely a moment since that time but that I was in the saddle, you may have some notion of the reason of my assent to this extraordinary proposition. Nor will I mention the doubts I had, as to the feasibility of the execution of this very novel proposal, except to say that I knew this morning that our larder was low; not to put too fine a point upon it, that we had nothing but some potatoes and sugar and coffee in the world.

And I may as well say here, that of such, in scant proportion, would have been our repast, had it not been for the
riding of miles by two persons, one an officer, to procure
supplies; and they only succeeded in getting some few chickens, some butter, and one huge loaf of bread, which last was
bought of a soldier, because he had grown faint in carrying
it, and was afterwards rescued with much difficulty and
after a long race from a four-footed hog, which had got hold
of and had actually eaten part of it. "There is a divinity," etc.
Suffice it, this very ingenious and unheard of contemplated
proceeding, first announced by the general, was accepted
and at once undertaken by his staff. Of the absolute quality
of what we had to eat, I could not pretend to judge, but I
think an unprejudiced person would have said of the bread
that it was good; so of the potatoes before they were boiled.
Of the chickens he would have questioned their age, but they
were large and in good *running* order. The toast was good
and the butter. There were those who, when coffee was given
them, called for tea, and vice versa, and were so ungracious
as to suggest that the water that was used in both might have
come from near a barn. Of course it did not. We all came
down to the little peach orchard where we had stayed last
night, and, wonderful to see and tell, ever mindful of our
needs, had it all ready, had our faithful John. There was an
enormous pan of stewed chickens, and the potatoes, and
toast, all hot, and the bread and the butter, and tea and
coffee. There was satisfaction derived from just naming
them all over. We called John an angel, and he snickered and

said he "knowed" we'd come. General Hancock is of course invited to partake, and without delay, we commence operations. Stools are not very numerous, two, in all, and these the two generals have by common consent. Our table was the top of a mess chest. By this the generals sat. The rest of us sat upon the ground, cross-legged, like the picture of a smoking Turk, and held our plates upon our laps. How delicious was the stewed chicken. I had a cucumber pickle in my saddle bags, the last of a lunch left there two or three days ago, which George brought, and I had half of it. We were just well at it when General Meade rode down to us from the line, accompanied by one of his staff, and by General Gibbon's invitation, they dismounted and joined us. For the general commanding the Army of the Potomac, George, by an effort worthy of the person and the occasion, finds an empty cracker box for a seat. The staff officer must sit upon the ground with the rest of us. Soon Generals Newton and Pleasanton, each with an aide, arrive. By an almost superhuman effort, a roll of blankets is found, which, upon a pinch, is long enough to seat these generals both, and room is made for them. The aides sit with us. And, fortunate to relate, there was enough cooked for us all, and from General Meade to the youngest second lieutenant we all had a most hearty and well-relished dinner. Of the "past" we were "secure." The generals ate, and after, lighted cigars, and under the flickering shade of a very small tree, discoursed of the incidents of yesterday's battle and of the probabilities of today. General Newton spoke humorously of General

Gibbon as "this young North Carolinian," and how he was becoming arrogant and above his position, because he commanded a corps. General Gibbon retorted by saying that General Newton had not been long enough in such a command, only since yesterday, to enable him to judge such things. General Meade still thought that the enemy would attack his left again today towards evening; but he was ready for them. General Hancock thought that the attack would be upon the position of the Second Corps. It was mentioned that General Hancock would again assume command of the Second Corps from that time, so that General Gibbon would again return to the Second Division.

General Meade spoke of the Provost Guards, that they were good men, and that it would be better today to have them in the works[7] than to stop stragglers and skulkers, as these latter would be good for but little even in the works; and so he gave the order that all the Provost Guards should at once temporarily rejoin their regiments. Then General Gibbon called up Captain Farrel, First Minnesota, who commanded the provost guard of his division, and directed him for that day to join the regiment. "Very well, sir," said the captain, as he touched his hat and turned away. He was a quiet, excellent gentleman and thorough soldier. I knew him well and esteemed him. I never saw him again. He was killed in two or three hours from that time, and over half of his splendid company were either killed or wounded.

---

7. Haskell probably wrote "ranks," as there were but few "works deserving the name on the field.—Ed.

And so the time passed on, each general now and then dispatching some order or message by an officer or orderly, until about half-past twelve, when all the generals, one by one, first General Meade, rode off their several ways, and General Gibbon and his staff alone remained.

We dozed in the heat, and lolled upon the ground, with half open eyes. Our horses were hitched to the trees munching some oats. A great lull rested upon all the field. Time was heavy, and for want of something better to do, I yawned and looked at my watch. It was five minutes before 1:00. I returned my watch to its pocket, and thought possibly that I might go to sleep, and stretched myself upon the ground accordingly. *Ex uno disce omnes*. My attitude and purpose were those of the general and the rest of the staff.

What sound was that? There was no mistaking it. The distinct sharp sound of one of the enemy's guns, square over to the front, caused us to open our eyes and turn them in that direction, when we saw directly above the crest the smoke of the bursting shell, and heard its noise. In an instant, before a word was spoken, as if that was the signal gun for general work, loud, startling, booming, the report of gun after gun in rapid succession smote our ears and their shells plunged down and exploded all around us. We sprang to our feet. In briefest time the whole Rebel line to the west was pouring out its thunder and its iron upon our devoted crest. The wildest confusion for a few moments obtained sway among us. The shells came bursting all about. The servants ran terror-stricken for dear life and disappeared. The horses, hitched to the trees or held by the slack hands of orderlies, neighed out in fright, broke away, and plunged riderless through the fields. The general at the first had snatched his sword, and started on foot for the front. I called for my horse; nobody responded. I found him tied to a tree, nearby, eating oats, with an air of the greatest composure, which under the circumstances, even then struck me as exceedingly ridiculous. He alone, of all beasts or men near, was cool. I am not sure but that I learned a lesson then from a horse. Anxious alone for his oats, while I put on the bridle and adjusted the halter, he delayed me by keeping his head down, so I had time to see one of the horses of our mess wagon struck and torn by a shell. The pair plunge—the driver has lost the reins—horses, driver, and wagon go into a heap by a tree. Two mules close at hand, packed with boxes of ammunition, are knocked all to prices by a shell. General Gibbon's groom has just mounted his horse and is starting to take the general's horse to him, when the flying iron meets him and tears open his breast. He drops dead and the horses gallop away. No more than a minute since the first shot was fired, and I am mounted and riding after the general. The mighty din that now rises to heaven and shakes the earth is not all of it the voice of the rebellion; for our guns, the guardian lions of the crest, quick to awake when danger comes, have opened their fiery jaws and begun to roar—the great hoarse roar of battle. I overtake the general half way up to the line. Before we reach the crest his horse is brought by an orderly. Leaving our horses just behind a sharp declivity of the ridge, on foot we go up among the batteries. How the long streams of fire spout from the guns, how the rifled shells hiss, how the smoke deepens and rolls. But where is the infantry? Has it vanished in smoke? Is this a nightmare or a juggler's devilish trick? All too real. The men of the infantry have seized their arms, and behind their works, behind every rock, in every ditch, wherever there is any shelter, they hug the ground, silent, quiet, unterrified, little harmed. The enemy's guns now in action are in position at their front of the woods along the second ridge that I have before mentioned and towards their right, behind a small crest in the open field, where we saw the flags this morning. Their line is some two miles long, concave on the side towards us, and their range is from 1,000 to 1,800 yards. A hundred and twenty-five rebel guns, we estimate, are now active, firing twenty-four pound, twenty-, twelve-, and ten-pound projectiles, solid shot and shells, spherical, conical, spiral. The enemy's fire is chiefly concentrated upon the position of the Second Corps. From the Cemetery to Round Top, with over 100 guns, and to all parts of the enemy's line, our batteries reply, of twenty- and ten-pound parrotts, ten-pound rifled ordnance, and twelve-pound napoleons, using projectiles as various in shape and name as those of the enemy. Captain Hazard commanding the artillery brigade of the Second Corps was vigilant among the batteries of his command, and they were all doing well. All was going on satisfactorily. We had nothing to do, therefore, but to be observers of the grand spectacle of battle. Captain Wessels, Judge Advocate of the division, now joined us, and we sat down behind the crest, close to the left of Cushing's Battery, to bide our time, to see, to be ready to act when the time should come, which might be at any moment.

Who can describe such a conflict as is raging around us? To say that it was like a summer storm, with the crash of thunder, the glare of lightning, the shrieking of the wind, and the clatter of hailstones, would be weak. The thunder and lightning of these 250 guns and their shells, whose smoke darkens the sky, is incessant, all pervading, in the air above our heads, on the ground at our feet, remote, near, deafening, ear piercing, astounding; and these hailstones are massy iron, charged with exploding fire. And there is little of human interest in a storm; it is an absorbing element of this. You may see flame and smoke, and hurrying men, and human passion at a great conflagration; but they are all earthly and nothing more. These guns are great infuriate demons, not of the earth, whose mouths blaze with smoky tongues of living fire, and whose murky breath, sulphur laden, rolls around them and along the ground, the smoke of Hades. These grimy men, rushing, shouting, their souls in frenzy, plying the dusky globes and the igniting spark, are in their league, and but their willing ministers. We thought that at the second Bull Run, at the Antietam and at Fredericksburg on the 11th of December, we had heard heavy cannonading; they were but holiday salutes compared with this. Besides the great ceaseless roar of the guns, which was but the background of the others, a million various minor sounds engaged the ear. The projectiles shriek long and sharp. They hiss, they scream, they growl, they sputter; all sounds of life and rage; and each has its different note, and all are discordant. Was ever such a chorus of sound before? We note the effect of the enemy's fire among the batteries and along the crest. We see the solid shot strike axle, or pole, or wheel, and the tough iron and heart of oak snap and fly like straws. The great oaks there by Woodruff's guns heave down their massy branches with a crash, as if the lighting smote them. The shells swoop down among the battery horses standing there apart. A half a dozen horses start, they stumble, their legs stiffen, their vitals and blood smear the ground. And these shot and shells have no respect for men either. We see the poor fellows hobbling back from the crest, or unable to do so, pale and weak, lying on the ground with the mangled stump of an arm or leg, dripping their lifeblood away; or with a cheek torn open, or a shoulder mashed. And many, alas! hear not the roar as they stretch upon the ground with upturned faces and open eyes, though a shell should burst at their very ears. Their ears and their bodies this instant are only mud. We saw them but a moment since there among the flame, with brawny arms and muscles of iron wielding the rammer and pushing home the cannon's plethoric load. Strange freaks these round shot play! We saw a man coming up from the rear with his full knapsack on, and some canteens of water held by the straps in his hands. He was walking slowly and with apparent unconcern, though the iron hailed around him. A shot struck the knapsack, and it, and its contents, flew thirty yards in every direction, the knapsack disappearing like an egg thrown spitefully against a rock. The soldier stopped and turned about in puzzled surprise, put up one hand to his back to assure himself that the knapsack was not there, and then walked slowly on again unharmed, with not even his coat torn. Near us was a man crouching behind a small disintegrated stone, which was about the size of a common water bucket. He was bent up, with his face to the ground, in the attitude of a Pagan worshipper before his idol. It looked so absurd to see him thus, that I went and said to him, "Do not lie there like a toad. Why not go to your regiment and be a man?" He turned up his face with a stupid, terrified look upon me, and then without a word turned his nose again to the ground. An orderly who was with me at the time told me that a few moments later, that a shot had struck the stone, smashing it in a thousand fragments, but did not touch the man, though his head was not six inches from the stone.

All the projectiles that came near us were not so harmless. Not ten yards away from us a shell burst among some small bushes, where sat three or four orderlies holding horses. Two of the men and one horse were killed. Only a few yards off, a shell exploded over an open limber box in Cushing's battery, and at the same instant, another shell over a neighboring box. In both the boxes, the ammunition blew up with an explosion that shook the ground, throwing fire and splinters and shells far into the air and all around, destroying several men. We watched the shells bursting in the air, as they came hissing in all directions. Their flash was a bright gleam of lightning radiating from a point, giving place in the thousandth part of a second to a small, white, puffy cloud, like a fleece of the lightest, whitest wool. These clouds were very numerous. We could not often see the shell before it burst; but sometimes, as we faced towards the enemy, and looked above our heads, the approach would be heralded by a prolonged hiss, which always seemed to me to be a line of something tangible, terminating in a black globe, distinct to the eye, as the sound had been to the ear. The shell would seem to stop, and hang suspended in the air an instant, and then vanish in fire and smoke and noise. We saw the missiles tear and plow the ground. All in rear of the crest for 1,000 yards, as well as among the batteries, was the field of their blind fury. Ambulances, passing down the Taney-town Road with wounded men, were struck. The hospitals near this road were riddled. The house which was General Meade's headquarters was shot through several times, and a great many horses of officers and orderlies were lying dead around it. Riderless horses, galloping madly through the fields, were brought up, or down rather, by these invisible horse tamers, and they would not run any more. Mules with ammunition, pigs wallowing about, cows in the pastures, whatever was animate or inanimate, in all this broad range, were no exception to their blind havoc. The percussion shells would strike, and thunder, and scatter the earth and their whistling fragments; the Whitworth bolts would pound and ricochet, and bowl far away sputtering, with the sound of a mass of hot iron plunged in water; and the great solid shot would smite the unresisting ground with a sounding "thud," as the strong boxer crashes his iron fist into the jaws of his unguarded adversary. Such were some of the sights and sounds of this great iron battle of missiles. Our artillerymen upon the crest budged not an inch, nor intermitted, but, though caisson and limber were smashed, and the guns dismantled, and men and horses killed, there amidst smoke and sweat, they gave back, without grudge, or loss of time in the sending, in kind whatever the enemy sent, globe, and cone, and bolt, hollow or solid, an iron greeting to the rebellion, the compliments of the wrathful Republic. An hour has droned its flight since first the war began. There is no sign of weariness or abatement on either side. So long it seemed, that the din and crashing around began to appear the normal condition of nature there, and fighting man's element. The general proposed to go among the men and over to the front of the batteries, so at about 2:00 he and I started. We went along the lines of the infantry as they lay there flat upon the earth, a little to the front of the batteries. They were suffering little, and were quiet and cool. How glad we were that the enemy were no better gunners, and that they cut the shell fuses too long. To the question asked the men, "What do you think of this?" the replies would be, "Oh, this is bully," "We are getting to like it," "Oh, we don't mind this." And so they lay under the heaviest cannonade that ever shook the continent, and among them a thousand times more jokes than heads were cracked.

We went down in front of the line some 200 yards, and as the smoke had a tendency to settle upon a higher plain than where we were, we could see near the ground distinctly all over the fields, as well back to the crest where were our own guns as to the opposite ridge where were those of the enemy. No infantry was in sight, save the skirmishers, and they stood silent and motionless—a row of gray posts through the field on one side confronted by another of blue. Under the grateful shade of some elm trees, where we could see much of the field, we made seats of the ground and sat down. Here all the more repulsive features of the fight were unseen, by reason of the smoke. Man had arranged the scenes, and for a time had taken part in the great drama; but at last, as the plot thickened, conscious of his littleness and inadequacy to the mighty part, he had stepped aside and given place to more powerful actors. So it seemed; for we could see no men about the batteries. On either crest we could see the great flaky streams of fire, and they seemed numberless, of the opposing guns, and their white banks of swift, convolving smoke; but the sound of the discharges was drowned in the universal ocean of sound. Over all the valley, the smoke, a sulphury arch, stretched its lurid span; and through it always, shrieking on their unseen courses, thickly flew myriad iron deaths. With our grim horizon on all sides round, toothed thick with battery flame, under that dissonant canopy of warring shells, we sat and heard in silence. What other expression had we that was not mean, for such an awful universe of battle?

A shell struck our breastwork of rails up in sight of us, and a moment afterwards we saw the men bearing some of their wounded companions away from the same spot; and directly two men came from there down toward where we were and sought to get shelter in an excavation nearby, where many dead horses, killed in yesterdays fight had been thrown. General Gibbon said to these men, more in a tone of kindly expostulation than of command "My men, do not leave your ranks to try to get shelter here. All these matters are in the hands of God, and nothing that you can do will make you safer in one place than in another." The men went quietly back to the line at once. The general then said to me: "I am not a member of any church, but I have always has a strong religious feeling; and so in all these battles I have always believed that I was in the hands of God, and that I should be unharmed or not, according to His will. For this reason, I think it is, I am always ready to go where duty calls, no matter how great the danger." Half past 2:00, an hour and a half since the commencement, and still the cannonade did not in the least abate; but soon thereafter some signs of weariness and a little slacking of fire began to be apparent upon both sides. First we saw Brown's battery retire from the line, too feeble for further battle. Its position was a little to the front of the line. Its commander was wounded, and many of its men were so, or worse; some of its guns had been disabled, many of its horses killed; its ammunition was nearly expended. Other batteries in similar case had been withdrawn before to be replaced by fresh ones, and some were withdrawn afterwards. Soon after the battery named had gone, the general and I started to return, passing towards the left of the division, and crossing the ground where the guns had stood. The stricken horses were numerous, and the dead and wounded men lay about, and as we passed these latter, their low, piteous call for water would invariably come to us, if they had yet any voice left. I found canteens of water near—no difficult matter where a battle has been—and held them to livid lips, and even in the faintness of death the eagerness to drink told of their terrible torture of thirst. But we must pass on. Our infantry was still unshaken, and in all the cannonade suffered very little. The batteries had been handled much more severely. I am unable to give any figures. A great number of horses had been killed, in some batteries more than half of all. Guns had been dismounted. A great many caissons, limbers and carriages had been destroyed, and usually from ten to twenty-five men to each battery had been struck, at least along our part of the crest. Altogether, the fire of the enemy had injured us much, both in the modes that I have stated and also by exhausting our ammunition and fouling our guns, so as to render our batteries unfit for further immediate use. The scenes that met our eyes on all hands among the batteries were fearful. All things must end, and the great cannonade was no exception to the general law of earth. In the number of guns active at one time, and in the duration or rapidity of their fire, this artillery engagement, up to this time, must stand alone and preeminent in this war. It has not been often, or many times, surpassed in the battles of the world. Two hundred and fifty guns, at least, rapidly fired for two mortal hours. Cipher out the number of tons of gunpowder and iron that made these two hours hideous.

Of the injury of our fire upon the enemy—except the facts that ours was the superior position, if not better served and constructed artillery, and that the enemy's artillery hereafter during the battle was almost silent—we know little. Of course, during the fight we often saw the enemy's caissons explode, and the trees rent by our shot crashing about his ears, but we can from these alone infer but little of general results. At 3:00 almost precisely, the last shot hummed and bounded and fell, and the cannonade was over. The purpose of General Lee in all this fire of his guns—we know it now, we did not at the time so well—was to disable our artillery and break up our infantry upon the position of the Second Corps, so as to render them less an impediment to the sweep of his own brigades and divisions over our crest and through our lines. He probably supposed our infantry was massed behind the crest and the batteries; and hence his fire was so high, and his fuses to the shells were cut so long, too long. The Rebel general failed in some of his plans in this behalf, as many generals have failed before and will again. The artillery fight over, men began to breathe more freely, and to ask, What next, I wonder? The battery men were among their guns, some leaning to rest and wipe the sweat from their sooty faces, some were handling ammunition boxes and replenishing those that were empty. Some batteries from the artillery reserve were moving up to take the places of the disabled ones; the smoke was clearing from the crests. There was a pause between acts, with the curtain down, soon to rise upon the final act, and catastrophe of Gettysburg. We have passed by the left of the Second Division, coming from the First; when we crossed the crest, the enemy was not in sight and all was still—we walked slowly along in the rear of the troops, by the ridge cut off now from a view of the enemy in his position, and were returning to the spot where we had left our horses. General Gibbon had just said that he inclined to the belief that the enemy was falling back, and that the cannonade was only one of his noisy modes of covering the movement. I said that I thought that fifteen minutes would show that, by all his bowling, the Rebel did not mean retreat. We were near our horses when we noticed Brigadier General Hunt, Chief of Artillery of the Army, near Woodruff's battery, swiftly moving about on horseback and, apparently in rapid manner, giving some orders about the guns. Thought we, What could this mean? In a moment afterwards, we met Captain Wessels and the orderlies who had our horses; they were on foot leading the horses. Captain Wessels was pale, and he said, excited, "General, they say the enemy's infantry is advancing." We sprang into our saddles, a score of bounds brought us upon the all-seeing crest. To say that men grew pale and held their breath at what we and they there saw, would not be true. Might not 6,000 men be brave and without shade of fear, and yet, before a hostile 18,000, armed, and not five min-

utes' march away, turn ashy white? None on that crest now
need be told that the enemy is advancing. Every eye could
see his legions, an overwhelming resistless tide of an ocean
of armed men sweeping upon us! Regiment after regiment,
and brigade after brigade, move from the woods and rapidly take their places in the lines forming the assault. Pickett's
proud division, with some additional troops, hold their
right; Pettigrew's (Worth's) their left. The first line at short
interval followed by a second, and that a third succeeds; and
columns between, support the lines. More than half a mile
their front extends; more than 1,000 yards the dull-gray
masses deploy, man touching man, rank pressing rank, and
line supporting line. The red flags wave, their horsemen gallop up and down; the arms of 18,000 men, barrel and bayonet, gleam in the sun, a sloping forest of flashing steel. Right
on they move, as with one soul, in perfect order, without
impediment of ditch, or wall or stream, over ridge and slope,
through orchard, and meadow, and cornfield, magnificent,
grim, irresistible. All was orderly and still upon our crest; no
noise and no confusion. The men had little need of commands, for the survivors of a dozen battles knew well
enough what this array in front portended, and, already in
their places, they would be prepared to act when the right
time should come. The click of the locks as each man raised
the hammer to feel with his fingers that the cap was on the
nipple; the sharp jar as a musket touched a stone upon the
wall when thrust in aiming over it, and the clicking of the
iron axles as the guns were rolled up by hand a little further

to the front, were quite all the sounds that could be heard. Cap boxes were slid around to the front of the body; cartridge boxes opened, officers opened their pistol holsters. Such preparations, little more was needed. The trefoil flags, colors of the brigades and divisions moved to their places in rear; but along the lines in front, the grand old ensign that first waved in battle at Saratoga in 1777, and which these people coming would rob of half its stars, stood up, and the west wind kissed it as the sergeants sloped its lance towards the enemy. I believe that not one above whom it then waved but blessed his God that he was loyal to it, and whose heart did not swell with pride towards it, as the emblem of the Republic before that treason's flaunting rag in front. General Gibbon rode down the lines, cool and calm, and in an unimpassioned voice he said to the men, "Do not hurry, men, and fire too fast, let them come up close before you fire, and then aim low and steadily." The coolness of their general was reflected in the faces of his men. Five minutes has elapsed since first the enemy have emerged from the woods—no great space of time surely, if measured by the usual standard by which men estimate duration—but it was long enough for us to note and weigh some of the elements of the mighty moment that surrounded us; the disparity of numbers between the assailants and the assailed; that few as were our numbers we could not be supported or reinforced until support would not be needed or would be too late; that upon the ability of the two trefoil divisions to hold the crest and repel the assault depended not only their own safety or destruction, but also the honor of the Army of the Potomac and defeat or victory at Gettysburg. Should these advancing men pierce our line and become the entering wedge, driven home, that would sever our army asunder, what hope would there be afterwards, and where the blood-earned fruits of yesterday? It was long enough for the Rebel storm to drift across more than half the space that had at first separated it from us. None, or all, of these considerations either depressed or elevated us. They might have done the former, had we been timid; the latter had we been confident and vain. But, we were there waiting, and ready to do our duty —that done, results could not dishonor us.

Our skirmishers open a spattering fire along the front, and, fighting, retire upon the main line—the first drops, the heralds of the storm, sounding on our windows. Then the thunders of our guns—first Arnold's, then Cushing's, and Woodruff's, and the rest — shake and reverberate again through the air, and their sounding shells smite the enemy. The general said I had better go and tell General Meade of this advance. To gallop to General Meade's headquarters, to learn there that he had changed them to another part of the field, to dispatch to him by the Signal Corps in General Gibbon's name the message, "The enemy is advancing his infantry in force upon my front," and to be again upon the crest, were but the work of a minute. All our available guns are now active, and from the fire of shells, as the range grows shorter and shorter, they change to shrapnel, and from shrapnel to canister; but in spite of shells, and shrapnel, and canister, without wavering or halt, the hardy lines of the enemy continue to move on. The Rebel guns make no reply to ours, and no charging shout rings out today, as is the Rebel wont; but the courage of these silent men amid our shots seems not to need the stimulus of other noise. The enemy's right flank sweeps near Stannard's bushy crest, and his concealed Vermonters rake it with a well-delivered fire of musketry. The gray lines do not halt or reply, but withdrawing a little from that extreme, they still move on. And so across all that broad open ground they have come, nearer and nearer, nearly half the way, with our guns bellowing in their faces, until now a hundred yards, no more, divide our ready left from their advancing right. The eager men there are impatient to begin. Let them. First, Harrow's breastworks flame; then Hall's; then Webb's. As if our bullets were the fire coals that touched off their muskets, the enemy in front halts, and his countless level barrels blaze back upon us. The Second Division is struggling in battle. The rattling storm soon spreads to the right, and the blue trefoils are viewing with the white. All along each hostile front, a thousand yards, with narrowest space between, the volleys blaze and roll; as thick the sound as when a summer hailstorm pelts the city roofs; as thick the fire as when the incessant lightning fringes a summer cloud. When the Rebel infantry had opened fire, our batteries soon became silent, and this without their fault, for they were foul by long previous use. They were the targets of the concentrated Rebel bullets, and some of them had expended all their canister. But they were not silent before Rhorty was killed, Woodruff had fallen mortally wounded, and Cushing, firing almost his last canister, had dropped dead among his guns shot through the head by a bullet. The conflict is left to the infantry alone. Unable to find my general when I had returned to the crest after transmitting his message to General Meade — and while riding in the search having witnessed the development of the fight, from the first fire upon the left by the main lines until all of the two divisions were furiously engaged — I gave up hunting as useless — I was convinced General Gibbon could not be on the field; I left him mounted; I could easily have found him now had he so remained; but now, save myself, there was not a mounted officer near the engaged lines — and was riding towards the right of the Second Division, with purpose to stop there, as the most eligible position to watch the further progress of the battle, there to be ready to take part according to my own notions whenever and wherever occasion was presented. The conflict was tremendous, but I had seen no wavering in all our line. Wondering how long the Rebel ranks, deep though they were, could stand our sheltered volleys, I had come near my destination, when — great heaven! Were my senses mad? The larger portion of Webb's brigade — my God, it was true — there by the group of trees and the angles of the wall, was breaking from the cover of their works, and, without orders or reason, with no hand lifted to check them, was falling back, a fear-stricken flock of confusion! The fate of Gettysburg hung upon a spider's single thread! A great magnificent passion came on me at the instant, not one that overpowers and confounds, but one that blanches the face and sublimes every sense and faculty. My sword, that had always hung idle by my side, the sign of rank only in every battle, I drew, bright and gleaming, the symbol of command. Was not that a fit occasion, and these fugitives the men on whom to try the temper of the Solinzen steel? All rules and proprieties were forgotten; all considerations of person, and danger and safety despised; for, as I met the tide of these rabbits, the damned red flags of the rebellion began to thicken and flaunt along the wall they had just deserted, and one was already waving over one of the guns of the dead Cushing. I ordered these men to "halt," and "face about," and "fire," and they heard my voice, and gathered my meaning, and obeyed my commands. On some unpatriotic backs of those not quick of comprehension, the flat of my sabre fell not lightly, and, at its touch, their love of country returned, and, with a look at me as if I were the destroying angel, as I might have become theirs, they again faced the enemy. General Webb soon came to my assistance. He was on foot, but he was active, and did all that one could do to repair the breach, or to avert its calamity. The men that had fallen back, facing the enemy, soon regained confidence in themselves, and became steady. This portion of the wall was lost to us, and the enemy had gained the cover of the reverse side, where he now stormed with fire. But Webb's men, with their bodies in part protected by the abruptness of the crest, now sent back in the enemy's face as fierce a storm. Some scores

of venturesome Rebels, that in their first push at the wall
had dared to cross at the further angle, and those that had
desecrated Cushing's guns, were promptly shot down, and
speedy death met him who should raise his body to cross it
again. At this point, little could be seen of the enemy, by
reason of his cover and the smoke, except the flash of his
muskets and his waving flags. These red flags were accumu-
lating at the wall every moment, and they maddened us as
the same color does the bull. Webb's men are falling fast,
and he is among them to direct and encourage; but, however well they may now do, with that walled enemy in front,
with more than a dozen flags to Webb's three, it soon
became apparent that in not many minutes they will be
overpowered, or that there will be none alive for the enemy
to overpower. Webb has but three regiments, all small, the
Sixt-ninth, Seventy-first, and Seventy-second Pennsylvania
—the Hundred-and-sixth Pennsylvania, except two companies, is not here today—and he must have speedy assistance,
or this crest will be lost. Oh, where is Gibbon? Where is
Hancock?—some general—anybody with the power and
the will to support that wasting, melting line? No general
came, and no succor! I thought of Hayes upon the right, but
from the smoke and war along his front, it was evident that
he had enough upon his hands, if he stayed the inrolling tide
of the Rebels there. Doubleday upon the left was too far off
and too slow, and on another occasion I had begged him to
send his idle regiments to support another line battling with
thrice its numbers, and this "Old Sumpter Hero" had

declined. As a last resort, I resolved to see if Hall and Harrow could not send some of their commands to reinforce Webb. I galloped to the left in the execution of my purpose, and as I attained the rear of Hall's line from the nature of the ground and the position of the enemy it was easy to discover the reason and the manner of this gathering of Rebel flags in front of Webb. The enemy, emboldened by his success in gaining our line by the group of trees and the angle of the wall, was concentrating all his right against and was further pressing that point. There was the stress of his assault; there would he drive his fiery wedge to split our line. In front of Harrow's and Hall's Brigades he had been able to advance no nearer than when he first halted to deliver fire, and these commands had not yielded an inch. To effect the concentration before Webb, the enemy would march the regiment on his extreme right of each of his lines by the left flank to the rear of the troops, still halted and facing to the front, and so continuing to draw in his right, when they were all massed in the position desired, he would again face them to the front, and advance to the storming. This was the way he made the wall before Webb's line blaze red with his battle flags, and such was the purpose there of his thick-crowding battalions. Not a moment must be lost. Colonel Hall I found just in rear of his line, sword in hand, cool, vigilant, noting all that passed and directing the battle of his brigade. The fire was constantly diminishing now in his front, in the manner and by the movement of the enemy that I have mentioned, drifting to the right.

"How is it going?" Colonel Hall asked me as I rode up.

"Well, but Webb is hotly pressed and must have support, or he will be overpowered. Can you assist him?"

"Yes."

"You cannot be too quick."

"I will move my brigade at once."

"Good."

He gave the order, and in briefest time I saw five friendly colors hurrying to the aid of the imperilled three; and each color represented true, battle-tried men, that had not turned back from Rebel fire that day nor yesterday, though their ranks were sadly thinned, to Webb's brigade, pressed back as it had been from the wall, the distance was not great from Hall's right. The regiments marched by the right flank. Colonel Hall superintended the movement in person. Colonel Devereux coolly commanded the Nineteenth Massachusetts. His major, Rice, had already been wounded and carried off. Lieutenant Colonel Macy, of the Twentieth Massachusetts, had just had his left hand shot off, and so Captain Abbott gallantly led over this fine regiment. The Forty-second New York followed their excellent Colonel Mallon. Lieutenant Colonel Steel, Seventh Michigan, had just been killed, and his regiment, and the handful of the Fifty-ninth New York, followed their colors. The movement, as it did, attracting the enemy's fire, and executed in haste, as it must be, was difficult; but in reasonable time, and in order that is serviceable, if not regular, Hall's men are fighting gallantly side by side with Webb's before the all-

important point. I did not stop to see all this movement of
Hall's, but from him I went at once further to the left, to the
First Brigade. General Harrow I did not see, but his fighting
men would answer my purpose as well. The Nineteenth
Maine, the Fifteenth Massachusetts, the Eighty-second New
York, and the shattered old thunderbolt, the First Minnesota—poor Farrell was dying then upon the ground where
he had fallen—all men that I could find I took over to the
right at the *double quick*.

As we were moving to, and near the other brigade of the
division, from my position on horseback, I could see that the
enemy's right, under Hall's fire, was beginning to stagger
and to break. "See," I said to the men, "See the *chivalry*! See
the gray-backs run!" The men saw, and as they swept to
their places by the side of Hall and opened fire, they roared,
and this in a manner that said more plainly than words—
for the deaf could have seen it in their faces, and the blind
could have heard it in their voices—*the crest is safe*!

The whole division concentrated, and changes of position, and new phases, as well on our part as on that of the
enemy, having as indicated occurred, for the purpose of
showing the exact present posture of affairs, some further
description is necessary. Before the Second Division the
enemy is massed; the main bulk of his force covered by the
ground that slopes to his rear, with his front at the stone
wall. Between his front and us extends the very apex of the
crest. All there is left of the White Trefoil Division—yesterday morning there were 3800, this morning there were

fewer than 3000—at this moment there are somewhat over 2000—twelve regiments in three brigades are below or behind the crest, in such a position that by the exposure of the head and upper part of the body above the crest they can deliver their fire in the enemy's face along the top of the wall. By reason of the disorganization incidental in Webb's brigade to his men's having broken and fallen back, as mentioned, in the two other brigades to their rapid and difficult change of position under fire, and in all the division in part to severe and continuous battle, formation of companies and regiments in regular ranks is lost; but commands, companies, regiments and brigades are blended and intermixed—an irregular extended mass—men enough, if in order, to form a line of four or five ranks along the whole front of the division. The twelve flags of the regiments wave defiantly at intervals along the front; at the stone wall, at unequal distances from ours of forty, fifty, or sixty yards, stream nearly double this number of the battle flags of the enemy. These changes accomplished on either side, and the concentration complete, although no cessation or abatement in the general din of conflict since the commencement had at any time been appreciable, now it was as if a new battle, deadlier, stormier than before, had sprung from the body of the old—a young Phoenix of combat, whose eyes stream lightning, shaking his arrowy wings over the yet glowing ashes of his progenitor. The jostling, swaying lines on either side boil, and roar, and dash their flaming spray, two hostile billows of a fiery ocean. Thick flashes stream from the wall, thick volleys answer from the crest. No threats or expostulation now, only example and encouragement. All depths of passion are stirred, and all combatives fire, down to their deep foundations. Individuality is drowned in a sea of clamor, and timid men, breathing the breath of the multitude, are brave. The frequent dead and wounded lie where they stagger and fall—there is no humanity for them now, and none can be spared to care for them. The men do not cheer or shout; they growl, and over that uneasy sea, heard with the roar of musketry, sweeps the muttered thunder of a storm of growls. Webb, Hall, Devereux, Mallon, Abbott among the men where all are heroes, are doing deeds of note. Now the loyal wave rolls up as if it would overleap its barrier, the crest. Pistols flash with the muskets. My "Forward to the wall" is answered by the Rebel counter command, "Steady, men!" and the wave swings back. Again it surges, and again it sinks. These men of Pennsylvania, on the soil of their own homesteads, the first and only to flee the wall, must be the first to storm it.

"Major, lead your men over the crest, they will follow."

"By the tactics I understand my place is in rear of the men."

"Your pardon, sir; I see *your* place is in rear of the men. I thought you were fit to lead."

"Captain Suplee, come on with your men."

"Let me first stop this fire in the rear, or we shall be hit by our own men."

"Never mind the fire in the rear; let us take care of this in front first."

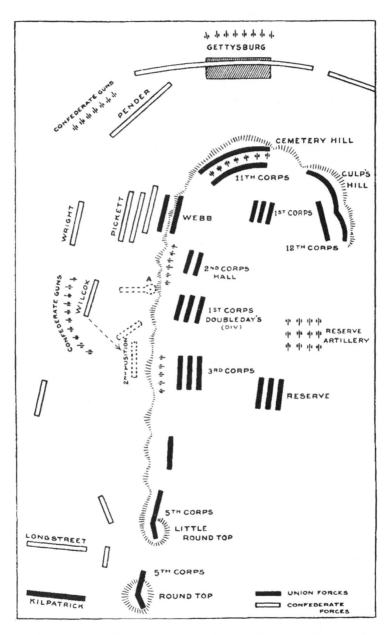

BATTLE OF GETTYSBURG — FINAL ATTACK, JULY 3
Compiled by C.E. Estabrook

"Sergeant, forward with your color. Let the Rebels see it close to their eyes once before they die."

The color sergeant of the Seventy-second Pennsylvania, grasping the stump of the severed lance in both his hands, waved the flag above his head and rushed towards the wall. "Will you see your color storm the wall alone?" One man only starts to follow. Almost half way to the wall, down go color bearer and color to the ground—the gallant sergeant is dead. The line springs—the crest of the solid ground with a great roar, heaves forward its maddened load, men, arms, smoke, fire, a fighting mass. It rolls to the wall—flash meets flash, the wall is crossed—a moment ensues of thrusts, yells, blows, shots, and undistinguishable conflict, followed by a shout universal that makes the welkin ring again, and the last and bloodiest fight of the great battle of Gettysburg is ended and won.

❀ ❀ ❀ ❀ ❀

Many things cannot be described by pen or pencil—such a fight is one. Some hints and incidents may be given, but a description or picture never. From what is told, the imagination may for itself construct the scene; otherwise he who never saw can have no adequate idea of what such a battle is.

When the vortex of battle passion had subsided, hopes, fears, rage, joy, of which the maddest and the noisiest was the last, and we were calm enough to look about us, we saw that, as with us, the fight with the Third Division was ended, and that in that division was a repetition of the scenes immediately about us. In that moment the judgment almost refused to credit the senses. Are these abject wretches about us, whom our men are now disarming and driving together in flocks, the jaunty men of Pickett's division, whose steady lines and flashing arms but a few moments since came sweeping up the slope to destroy us? Are these red cloths that our men toss about in derision the "fiery Southern crosses," thrice ardent, the battle flags of the rebellion that waved defiance at the wall? We know, but so sudden has been the transition, we yet can scarce believe.

Just as the fight was over, and the first outburst of victory had a little subsided, when all in front of the crest was noise and confusion—prisoners being collected, small parties in pursuit of them far down into the fields, flags waving, officers giving quick, sharp commands to their men—I stood apart for a few moments upon the crest, by that group of trees which ought to be historic forever, a spectator of the thrilling scene around. Some few musket shots were still heard in the Third Division; and the enemy's guns, almost silent since the advance of his infantry until the moment of his defeat, were dropping a few sullen shells among friend and foe upon the crest. Rebellion fosters such humanity. Near me, saddest sight of the many of such a field and not in keeping with all this noise, were mingled alone the thick dead of Maine and Minnesota, and Michigan and Massachusetts, and the Empire and Keystone states, who, not yet cold, with the blood still oozing from their death-wounds, had given their lives to the country upon that stormy field.

So mingled upon that crest, let their honored graves be. Look with me about us. These dead have been avenged already. Where the long lines of the enemy's thousands so proudly advanced, see how thick the silent men of gray are scattered. It is not an hour since these legions were sweeping along so grandly; now 1,600 [8] of that fiery mass are strewn among the trampled grass, dead as the clods they load; more than 7,000, probably 8,000, are wounded, some there with the dead, in our hands, some fugitive far towards the woods, among them Generals Pettigrew, Garnett, Kemper, and Armstead, the last three mortally, and the last one in our hands. "Tell General Hancock," he said to Lieutenant Mitchell, Hancock's aide-de-camp, to whom he handed his watch, "that I know I did my country a great wrong when I took up arms against her, for which I am sorry, but for which I cannot live to atone." Four thousand, not wounded, are prisoners of war. More in number of the captured than the captors. Our men are still "gathering them in." Some hold up their hands or a handkerchief in sign of submission; some have hugged the ground to escape our bullets and so are taken; few made resistance after the first moment of our crossing the wall; some yield submissively with good grace, some with grim, dogged aspect, showing that but for the other alternative they could not submit to this. Colonels, and all less grades of officers, in the usual proportion are among them, and all are being stripped of their arms. Such

8. Final returns gave 1,653 buried by the First and Second Corps, presumably in this field. See 43 War Records, 264, 378.—ED.

of them as escaped wounds and capture are fleeing routed and panic stricken, and disappearing in the woods. Small arms, more thousands than we can count, are in our hands, scattered over the field. And these defiant battle flags, some inscribed with "First Manassas," the numerous battles of the Peninsula, "Second Manassas," "South Mountain," "Sharpsburg" (our Antietam), "Fredericksburg," "Chancellorsville," and many more names, our men have, and are showing about, *over thirty of them.*

Such was really the closing scene of the grand drama of Gettysburg. After repeated assaults upon the right and the left, where, and in all of which repulse had been his only success, this persistent and presuming enemy forms his chosen troops, the flower of his army, for a grand assault upon our center. The manner and result of such assault have been told—a loss to the enemy of from 12,000 to 14,000, killed, wounded and prisoners, and of over thirty battle flags. This was accomplished by not over six thousand men, with a loss on our part of not over 2,500 killed and wounded.

Would to Heaven Generals Hancock and Gibbon could have stood there where I did, and have looked upon that field! It would have done two men, to whom the country owes much, good to have been with their men in that moment of victory—to have seen the result of those dispositions which they had made, and of that splendid fighting which men schooled by their discipline, had executed. But they are both severely wounded and have been carried from the field. One person did come then that I was glad to see there, and that was no less than Major General Meade, whom the Army of the Potomac was fortunate enough to have at that time to command it. See how a great general looked upon the field, and what he said and did at the moment, and when he learned of his great victory. To appreciate the incident I give, it should be borne in mind that one coming up from the rear of the line, as did General Meade, could have seen very little of our own men, who had now crossed the crest, and although he could have heard the noise, he could not have told its occasion, or by whom made, until he had actually attained the crest. One who did not know results, so coming, would have been quite as likely to have supposed that our line there had been carried and captured by the enemy—so many gray Rebels were on the crest—as to have discovered the real truth. Such mistake was really made by one of our officers, as I shall relate.

General Meade rode up, accompanied alone by his son, who is his aide-de-camp, an escort, if select, not large for a commander of such an army. The principal horseman was no bedizened hero of some holiday review, but he was a plain man, dressed in a serviceable summer suit of dark blue cloth, without badge or ornament, save the shoulder straps of his grade, and a light, straight sword of a general or general staff officer. He wore heavy, high-top boots and buff gauntlets, and his soft black felt hat was slouched down over his eyes. His face was very white, not pale, and the lines were marked and earnest and full of care. As he arrived near me, coming up the hill, he asked in a sharp, eager voice: "How is it going here?" "I believe, general, the enemy's attack is repulsed," I answered. Still approaching, and a new light began to come in his face, of gratified surprise, with a touch of incredulity, of which his voice was also the medium, he further asked: "*What! Is the assault already repulsed?*" his voice quicker and more eager than before. "It is, sir," I replied. By this time he was on the crest, and when his eye had for an instant swept over the field, taking in just a glance of the whole—the masses of prisoners, the numerous captured flags which the men were derisively flaunting about, the fugitives of the routed enemy, disappearing with the speed of terror in the woods—partly at what I had told him, partly at what he saw, he said, impressively, and his face lighted: "Thank God." And then his right hand moved as if it would have caught off his hat and waved it; but this gesture he suppressed, and instead he waved his hand, and said, "Hurrah!" The son, with more youth in his blood and less rank upon his shoulders, snatched off his cap, and roared out his three "hurrahs" right heartily. The general then surveyed the field, some minutes, in silence. He at length asked who was in command—he had heard that Hancock and Gibbon were wounded—and I told him that General Caldwell was the senior officer of the corps and General Harrow of the division. He asked where they were, but before I had time to answer that I did not know, he resumed: "No matter; I will give my orders to you and you will see them executed." He then gave direction that the troops should be reformed as soon as practicable, and kept in their places, as the enemy might be mad enough to attack again. He also gave directions concerning the posting of some reinforcements which he said would soon be there, adding: "If the enemy does attack, charge him in the flank and sweep him from the field; do you understand." The general then, a gratified man, galloped in the direction of his headquarters.

Then the work of the field went on. First, the prisoners were collected and sent to the rear. "There go the men," the Rebels were heard to say, by some of our surgeons who were in Gettysburg, at the time Pickett's division marched out to take position—"There go the men that will go through your d——d Yankee lines, for you." A good many of them did "go through our lines for us," but in a very different way from the one they intended—not impetuous victors, sweeping away our thin lines with ball and bayonet, but crestfallen captives, without arms, guarded by the true bayonets of the Union, with the cheers of their conquerors ringing in their ears. There was a grim truth after all in this Rebel remark. Collected, the prisoners began their dreary march, a miserable, melancholy stream of dirty gray, to pour over the crest to our rear. Many of the officers were well-dressed, fine, proud gentlemen, such men as it would be a pleasure to meet, when the war is over. I had no desire to exult over them, and pity and sympathy were the general feelings of us all upon the occasion. The cheering of our men, and the unceremonious handling of the captured flags was probably not gratifying to the prisoners, but not intended for taunt or

insult to the men; they could take no exception to such prac-
tices. When the prisoners were turned to the rear and were
crossing the crest, Lieutenant Colonel Morgan, General
Hancock's Chief of Staff, was conducting a battery from the
artillery reserve, towards the Second Corps. As he saw the
men in gray coming over the hill, he said to the officer in
command of the battery: "See up there! The enemy has carried the crest. See them come pouring over! The old Second
Corps is gone, and you had better get your battery away
from here as quickly as possible, or it will be captured." The
officer was actually giving the order to his men to move
back, when close observation discovered that the gray-backs
that were coming had no arms, and then the truth flashed
upon the minds of the observers. The same mistake was
made by others.

In view of the results of that day—the successes of the
arms of the country, would not the people of the whole
country, standing there upon the crest with General Meade,
have said with him, "Thank God?"

I have no knowledge and little notion of how long a time
elapsed from the moment the fire of the infantry commenced, until the enemy was entirely repulsed, in this his
grand assault. I judge, from the amount of fighting and the
changes of position that occurred, that probably the fight
was of nearly an hour's duration, but I cannot tell, and I
have seen none who knew. The time seemed but a very few
minutes when the battle was over.

When the prisoners were cleared away and order was

again established upon our crest, where the conflict had impaired it, until between 5:00 and 6:00, I remained upon the field, directing some troops to their position, in conformity to the orders of General Meade. The enemy appeared no more in front of the Second Corps; but while I was engaged as I have mentioned, farther to our left some considerable force of the enemy moved out and made show of attack. Our artillery, now in good order again, in due time opened fire, and the shells scattered the "Butternuts," as clubs do the gray snowbirds of winter, before they came within range of our infantry. This, save unimportant outpost firing, was the last of the battle.

Of the pursuit of the enemy and the movements of the army subsequent to the battle, until the crossing of the Potomac by Lee and the closing of the campaign, it is not my purpose to write. Suffice it that on the night of the 3rd of July the enemy withdrew his left, Ewell's Corps, from our front, and on the morning of the 4th we again occupied the village of Gettysburg, and on that national day victory was proclaimed to the country; that floods of rain on that day prevented army movements of any considerable magnitude, the day being passed by our army in position upon the field, in burying our dead, and some of those of the enemy, and in making the movements already indicated; that on the 5th the pursuit of the enemy was commenced—his dead were buried by us—and the corps of our army, upon various roads, moved from the battlefield.

With a statement of some of the results of the battle, as to losses and captures, and of what I saw in riding over the field when the enemy was gone, my account is done.

Our own losses in killed, wounded and missing I estimate at 23,000.[9] Of the "missing" the larger proportion were prisoners, lost on the 1st of July. Our loss in prisoners, not wounded, probably was 4,000. The losses were distributed among the different army corps about as follows: In the Second Corps, which sustained the heaviest loss of any corps, a little over 4,500, of whom the missing were a mere nominal number; in the First Corps a little over 4,000, of whom a great many were missing; in the Third Corps 4,000, of whom some were missing; in the Eleventh Corps nearly 4,000, of whom the most were missing; and the rest of the loss, to make the aggregate mentioned, was shared by the Fifth, Sixth, and Twelfth Corps and the cavalry. Among these the missing were few; and the losses of the Sixth Corps and of the cavalry were light. I do not think the official reports will show my estimate of our losses to be far from correct, for I have taken great pains to questions staff officers upon the subject, and have learned approximate numbers from them. We lost no gun or flag that I have heard of in all the battle. Some small arms, I suppose, were lost on the 1st of July.

---

9. Final returns stated the loss as 23,049, as follows: First Corps, 3,897 killed and wounded, 2,162 missing; Second Corps, 3,991 and 387; Third Corps, 3,622 and 589; Fifth Corps, 1,976 and 211; Sixth Corps, 212 and 30; Eleventh Corps, 2,291 and 1,510; Twelfth Corps, 1,016 and 66; Artillery Reserve, 230 and 12; Cavalry, 445 and 407. See 43 War Records, 187.—ED.

The enemy's loss in killed, wounded, and prisoners I estimate at 40,000, and from the following data and for the following reasons: So far as I can learn, we took 10,000 prisoners, who were not wounded—many more than these were captured, but several thousands of them were wounded. I have so far as practicable ascertained the number of dead the enemy left upon the field, approximately, by getting the reports of different burying parties. I think his dead upon the field were 5,000, almost all of whom, save those killed on the first of July, were buried by us—the enemy not having them in their possession. In looking at a great number of tables of killed and wounded in battles I have found that the proportion of the killed to the wounded is as one to five, or more than five, rarely less than five. So with the killed at the number stated, 25,000 mentioned. I think 14,000 of the enemy, wounded and unwounded, fell into our hands. Great numbers of his small arms, two or three guns, and forty or more—was there ever such bannered harvest?—of his regimental battle flags, were captured by us. Someday possibly we may learn the enemy's loss, but I doubt if he will ever tell truly how many flags he did not take home with him. I have great confidence however in my estimates, for they have been carefully made, and after much inquiry, and with no desire or motive to overestimate the enemy's loss.

The magnitude of the armies engaged, the number of the casualties, the object sought by the Rebel, the result, will all contribute to give Gettysburg a place among the great historic battles of the world. That General Meade's concentration was rapid—over thirty miles a day was marched by some of the Corps—that his position was skillfully selected and his dispositions good; that he fought the battle hard and well; that his victory was brilliant and complete, I think all should admit. I cannot but regard it as highly fortunate to us and commendable in General Meade, that the enemy was allowed the initiative, the offensive, in the main battle; that it was much better to allow the Rebel, for his own destruction, to come up and smash his lines and columns upon the defensive solidity of our position, than it would have been to hunt him, for the same purpose, in the woods, or to unearth him from his rifle pits. In this manner our losses were lighter, and his heavier, than if the case had been reversed. And whatever the books may say of troops fighting the better who makes the attack, I am satisfied that in this war, Americans, the Rebels, as well as ourselves, are best on the defensive. The proposition is deducible from the battles of the war, I think, and my own observation confirms it.

But men there are who think that nothing was gained or done well in this battle, because some other general did not have the command, or because any portion of the army of the enemy was permitted to escape capture or destruction. As if one army of a 100,000 men could encounter another of the same number of as good troops and annihilate it! Military men do not claim or expect this; but the McClellan destroyers do, the doughty knights of purchasable newspaper quills; the formidable warriors from the brothels of politics, men of much warlike experience against honesty and honor, of profound attainments in ignorance, who have the maxims of Napoleon, whose spirit they as little understand as they most things, to quote, to prove all things; but who, unfortunately, have much influence in the country and with the government, and so over the army. It is very pleasant for these people, no doubt, at safe distances from guns, in the enjoyment of a lucrative office, or of a fraudulently obtained government contract, surrounded by the luxuries of their own firesides, where mud and flooding storms, and utter weariness never penetrate, to discourse of battles and how campaigns should be conducted and armies of the enemy destroyed. But it should be enough, perhaps, to say that men here, or elsewhere, who have knowledge enough of military affairs to entitle them to express an opinion on such matters, and accurate information enough to realize the nature and the means of this desired destruction of Lee's army before it crossed the Potomac into Virginia, will be most likely to vindicate the Pennsylvania campaign of General Meade, and to see that he accomplished all that could have been reasonably expected of any general of any army. Complaint has been, and is, made specially against Meade, that he did not attack Lee near Williamsport before he had time to withdraw across the river. These were the facts concerning this matter:

The 13th of July was the earliest day when such an attack, if practicable at all, could have been made. The time before this, since the battle, had been spent in moving the army from the vicinity of the field, finding something of the enemy and concentrating before him. On that day, the army was concentrated and in order of battle near the turnpike that leads from Sharpsburg to Hagerstown, Maryland, the right resting at or near the latter place, the left near Jones's crossroads, some six miles in the direction of Sharpsburg, and in the following order from left to right: the Twelfth Corps, the Second, the Fifth, the Sixth, the First, the Eleventh; the Third being in reserve behind the Second. The mean distance to the Potomac was some six miles, and the enemy was between Meade and the river. The Potomac, swelled by the recent rain, was boiling and swift and deep, a magnificent place to have drowned all the Rebel crew. I have not the least doubt but that General Meade would have liked to drown them all, if he could, but they were unwilling to be drowned, and would fight first. To drive them into the river then, they must be routed. General Meade, I believe, favored an attack upon the enemy at that time, and he summoned his corps commanders to a council upon the subject. The First Corps was represented by William Hayes, the Third by French, the Fifth by Sykes, the Sixth by Sedgwick, the Eleventh by Howard, the Twelfth by Slocum, and the Cavalry by Pleasanton. Of the eight generals there, Wadsworth, Howard and Pleasanton were in favor of immediate attack, and five, Hayes, French, Sykes, Sedgwick and Slocum were not in favor of attack until better information was obtained of the position and situation of the enemy. Of the *pros,* Wadsworth only temporarily represented the First

Corps in the brief absence of Newton, who, had a battle occurred, would have commanded. Pleasanton, with his horses, would have been a spectator only, and Howard, with the *brilliant Eleventh Corps*, would have been trusted nowhere but a safe distance from the enemy—not by General Howard's fault, however, for he is a good and brave man. Such was the position of those who felt sanguinarily inclined. Of the cons were all of the fighting generals of the fighting corps, save the First. This, then, was the feeling of these generals—all who would have had no responsibility or part in all probability, *hankered* for a fight—those who would have had both part and responsibility, did not. The attack was not made. At daylight on the morning of the 14th, strong reconnaissances from the Twelfth, Second and Fifth corps were the means of discovering that between the enemy, except a thousand of 1,500 of his rear guard, who fell into our hands, and the Army of the Potomac, rolled the rapid, unbridged river. The Rebel general, Pettigrew, was here killed. The enemy had constructed bridges, had crossed during all the preceding night, but so close were our cavalry and infantry upon him in the morning, that the bridges were destroyed before his rear guard had all crossed.

Among the considerations influencing these generals against the propriety of attack at that time, were probably the following: The army was wearied and worn down by four weeks of constant forced marching or battle, in the midst of heat, mud, and drenching showers, burdened with arms, accoutrements, blankets, sixty to a hundred cartridges, and five to eight days' rations. What such weariness means few save soldiers know. Since the battle, the army had been constantly diminished by sickness or prostration and by more straggling than I ever saw before. Poor fellows— they could not help it. The men were near the point when further efficient physical exertion was quite impossible. Even the sound of the skirmishing, which was almost constant, and the excitement of impending battle, had no effect to arouse for an hour the exhibition of their wonted former vigor. The enemy's loss in battle, it is true, had been far heavier than ours; but his army was less weary than ours, for in a given time since the first of the campaign, it had marched far less and with lighter loads. These Rebels are accustomed to hunger and nakedness, customs to which our men do not take readily. And the enemy had straggled less, for the men were going away from battle and towards home, and for them to straggle was to go into captivity, whose end they could not conjecture. The enemy was somewhere in position in a ridgy, wooded country, abounding in strong defensive positions, his main bodies concealed, protected by rifle pits and epaulements, acting strictly on the defensive. His dispositions, his position even, with any considerable degree of accuracy was unknown, nor could they be known except by reconnaissances in such force, and carried to such extent, as would have constituted them attacks liable to bring on at any moment a general engagement, and at places where we were least prepared and least likely to be successful. To have had a battle there then, General Meade would have had to

attack a cunning enemy in the dark, where surprises, undis-
covered rifle pits and batteries, and unseen bodies of men
might have met his forces at every point. With his not
greatly superior numbers, under such circumstances had
General Meade attacked, would he have been victorious?
The vote of these generals at the council shows their opinion—my own is that he would have been repulsed with
heavy loss, with little damage to the enemy. Such a result
might have satisfied the bloody politicians better than the
end of the campaign as it was; but I think the country did
not need that sacrifice of the Army of the Potomac at that
time—that enough odor of sacrifice came up to its nostrils
from the First Fredericksburg field, to stop their snuffing for
some time. I felt the probability of defeat strongly at the
time, when we all supposed that a conflict would certainly
ensue; for always before a battle—at least it so happens to
me—some dim presentiment of result, some unaccountable
foreshadowing pervades the army. I never knew the result to
prove it untrue, which rests with the weight of a conviction.
Whether such shadows are cause or consequence, I shall not
pretend to determine; but when, as they often are, they are
general, I think they should not be wholly disregarded by
the commander. I believe the Army of the Potomac is always
willing, often eager, to fight the enemy, whenever, as it
thinks, there is a fair chance for victory; that it always will
fight, let come victory or defeat whenever it is ordered so to
do. Of course the army, both officers and men, had very
great disappointment and very great sorrow that the Rebels

escaped—so it was called—across the river; the disappointment was genuine, at least to the extent that disappointment
is like surprise; but the sorrow to judge by looks, tones, and
actions, rather than by words, was not of that deep, sable
character for which there is no balm.

Would it be an imputation upon the courage or patriotism of this army if it was not rampant for fight at this particular time and under the existing circumstances? Had the
enemy stayed upon the left bank of the Potomac twelve
hours longer, there would have been a great battle there near
Williamsport on the 14th of July.

After such digression, if such it is, I return to Gettysburg.

As good generalship is claimed for General Meade in the
battle, so was the conduct of his subordinate commanders
good. I know, and have heard, of no bad conduct or blun-
dering on the part of any officer, save that of Sickles, on the
2nd of July, and that was so gross, and came so near being
the cause of irreparable disaster that I cannot discuss it with
moderation. I hope the man may never return to the Army
of the Potomac, or elsewhere, to a position where his inca-
pacity, or something worse, may bring fruitless destruction
to thousands again. The conduct of officers and men was
good. The Eleventh corps behaved badly; but I have yet to
learn the occasion when, in the opinion of any save their
own officers and themselves, the men of this corps have
behaved well on the march or before the enemy, either under
Siegel or any other commander. With this exception, and
some minor cases of very little consequence in the general

result, our troops whenever and wherever the enemy came, stood against them storms of impassable fire. Such was the infantry, such the artillery—the cavalry did less but it did all that was required.

The enemy, too, showed a determination and valor worthy of a better cause. Their conduct in this battle even makes me proud of them as Americans. They would have been victorious over any but the best of soldiers. Lee and his generals presumed too much upon some past successes, and did not estimate how much they were due on their part to position, as at Fredericksburg, or on our part to bad generalship, as at the Second Bull Run and Chancellorsville.

The fight of the 1st of July we do not, of course, claim as a victory; but even that probably would have resulted differently had Reynolds not been struck. The success of the enemy in the battle ended with the 1st of July. The Rebels were joyous and jubilant—so said our men in their hands, and the citizens of Gettysburg—at their achievements on that day. Fredericksburg and Chancellorsville were remembered by them. They saw victory already won, or only to be snatched from the streaming coat-tails of the Eleventh Corps, or the *raw Pennsylvania militia* as they thought they were, when they saw them run; and already the spires of Baltimore and the dome of the National Capitol were forecast upon their glad vision—only two or three days' march away through the beautiful valleys of Pennsylvania and *my* Maryland. Was there ever anything so fine before? How splendid it would be to enjoy the poultry and the fruit, the meats, the cakes, the beds, the clothing, the *whiskey* without price in this rich land of the Yankee! It would, indeed! But on the 2nd of July something of a change came over the spirit of these dreams. They were surprised at results and talked less and thought more as they prepared supper that night. After the fight of the 3rd they talked only of the means of their own safety from destruction. Pickett's splendid division had been almost annihilated, they said, and they talked not of how many were lost, but of who had escaped. They talked of these "Yanks" that had *clubs* on their flags and caps, the trefoils of the Second Corps that are like *clubs* in cards. The battle of Gettysburg is distinguished in this war, not only as by far the greatest and severest conflict that has occurred, but for some other things that I may mention. The fight of the 2nd of July, on the left, which was almost a separate and complete battle, is, so far as I know, alone in the following particulars: the numbers of men actually engaged at one time, and the enormous losses that occurred in killed and wounded in the space of about two hours. If the truth could be obtained, it would probably show a much larger number of casualties in this than my estimate in a former part of these sheets. Few battles of the war that have had so many casualties altogether as those of the two hours on the 2nd of July. The 3rd of July is distinguished. Then occurred the "great cannonade"— so we call it, and so it would be called in any war, and in almost any battle. And besides this, the main operations that followed have few parallels in history, none in this war, of the magnitude and magnificence of the assault, single and simultaneous, the disparity of the numbers engaged, and the brilliancy, completeness and overwhelming character of the result in favor of the side numerically the weaker. I think I have not, in giving the results of this encounter, overestimated the numbers or the losses of the enemy. We learned on all hands, by prisoners and by the newspapers, that over two divisions moved up to the assault—Pickett's and Pettigrew's—that this was the first engagement of Pickett's in the battle, and the first of Pettigrew's, save a light participation on the 1st of July. The Rebel divisions usually number nine or then thousand, or did at that time, as we understood. Then I have seen something of troops and think I can estimate their numbers somewhat. The number of the Rebels killed here I have estimated in this way: the Second and Third divisions of the Second Corps buried the Rebel dead in their own front, and where they fought upon their own grounds, by count they buried over 1,800. I think no more than about 200 of these were killed on the 2nd of July in front of the Second Division, and the rest must have fallen upon the 3rd. My estimates that depend upon this contingency may be erroneous, but to no great extent. The rest of the particulars of the assault, our own losses and our captures, I know are approximately accurate. Yet the whole sounds like romance, a grand stage piece of blood.

Of all the *corps d'armie*, for hard fighting, severe losses and brilliant results, the palm should be, as by the army it is, awarded to the *Old Second*. It did more fighting than any other corps, inflicted severer losses upon the enemy in killed and wounded, and sustained a heavier life loss, and captured more flags than all the rest of the army, and almost as many prisoners as the rest of the army. The loss of the Second Corps in killed and wounded in this battle—there is no other test of hard fighting—was almost as great as that of all General Grant's forces in the battle that preceded and in the siege of Vicksburg. Three-eighths of the whole corps were killed and wounded. Why does the Western Army suppose that the Army of the Potomac does not fight? Was ever a more absurd supposition? The Army of the Potomac is grand! Give it good leadership—let it alone—and it will not fail to accomplish all that reasonable men desire.

Of Gibbon's white trefoil division, if I am not cautious, I shall speak too enthusiastically. This division has been accustomed to distinguished leadership. Sumner, Sedgwick, and Howard have honored, and been honored by, its command. It was repulsed under Sedgwick at Antietam and under Howard at Fredericksburg; it was victorious under Gibbon at the Second Fredericksburg and at Gettysburg. At Gettysburg its loss in killed and wounded was over *1,700*, near one-half of all engaged; it captured *17* battle flags and *2,300* prisoners. Its bullets hailed on Pickett's division, and killed or mortally wounded four Rebel generals, Barksdale on the 2nd of July, with the three on the 3rd, *Armstead*, *Garnett*, and *Kemper*. In losses, in killed and wounded, and in captures from the enemy of prisoners and flags, it stood preeminent among all the divisions at Gettysburg.

Under such generals as Hancock and Gibbon, brilliant results may be expected. Will the country remember them?

It is understood in the army that the President thanked the slayer of Barton Key for *saving the day* at Gettysburg. Does the country know any better than the President, that Meade, Hancock, and Gibbon were entitled to some little share of such credit?

At about 6:00 on the afternoon of the 3rd of July, my duties done upon the field, I quitted it to go to the general. My brave horse Dick—poor creature, his good conduct in the battle that afternoon had been complimented by a brigadier—was a sight to see. He was literally covered with blood. Struck repeatedly, his right thigh had been ripped open in a ghastly manner by a piece of shell, and three bullets were lodged deep in his body, and from his wounds, the blood oozed and ran down his sides and legs and with the sweat, formed a bloody foam. Dick's was no mean part in that battle. Good conduct in men under such circumstances as he was placed in might result from a sense of duty—his was the result of his bravery. Most horses would have been unmanageable with the flash and roar of arms about and the shouting. Dick was utterly cool, and would have obeyed the rein had it been a straw. To Dick belongs the honor of first mounting that stormy crest before the enemy, not forty yards away, whose bullets smote him, and of being the only horse there during the heat of the battle. Even the enemy noticed Dick, and one of their reports of the battle mentions the "solitary horseman" who rallied our wavering line. He enabled me to do twelve times as much as I could have done on foot. It would not be dignified for an officer on foot to run; it is entirely so, mounted, to gallop. I do not approve of officers dismounting in battle, which is the time of all when they most need to be mounted, for thereby they have so much greater facilities for being everywhere present. Most officers, however, in close action, dismount. Dick deserves well of his country, and one day should have a horse monument. If there be *ut sapientibus placit*, and equine elysium, I will send to Charon the brass coin, the fee for Dick's passage over, and on the other side of the Styx in those shadowy clover fields he may nibble blossoms forever.

I had been struck upon the thigh by a bullet which I think must have glanced and partially spent its force upon my saddle. It had pierced the thick cloth of my trousers and two thicknesses of underclothing, but had not broken the skin, leaving me with an enormous bruise that for a time benumbed the entire leg. At the time of receiving it, I heard the thump, and noticed it and the hole in the cloth into which I thrust my finger, and I experienced a feeling of relief, I am sure, when I found that my leg was not pierced. I think when I dismounted my horse after that fight that I was no very comely specimen of humanity. Drenched with sweat, the white of battle, by the reaction, now turned to burning red. I felt like a boiled man; and had it not been for the exhilaration at results, I should have been miserable. This kept me up, however, and having found a man to transfer the saddle from poor Dick, who was now disposed to lie down by loss of blood and exhaustion, to another horse, I hobbled on among the hospitals in search of General Gibbon.

The skulkers were about, and they were as loud as any in their rejoicings at the victory, and I took a malicious pleasure as I went along and met them, in taunting the *sneak*s with their cowardice and telling them—it was not true— that General Meade had just given the order to the Provost Guard to arrest and shoot all men they could find away from their regiments who could not prove a good account of themselves. To find the general was no easy matter. I inquired for both Generals Hancock and Gibbon—I knew well enough that they would be together—and for the hospitals of the Second Corps. My search was attended with many incidents that were provokingly humorous. The stupidity of most men is amazing. I would ask of a man I met, "Do you know, sir, where the Second Corps hospitals are?" "The Twelfth Corps hospital is there!" Then I would ask sharply, "Did you understand me to ask for the Twelfth Corps hospital?" "No!" "Then why tell me what I do not ask or care to know?" Then stupidity would stare or mutter about the ingratitude of some people for kindness. Did I ask for the generals I was looking for, they would announce the interesting fact, in reply, that they had seen some other generals. Some were sure that General Hancock or Gibbon was dead. They had seen his dead body. This was a falsehood, and they knew it. Then it was General Longstreet. This was also, as they knew, a falsehood.

Oh, sorrowful was the sight to see so many wounded!

The whole neighborhood in rear of the field became one vast hospital of miles in extent. Some could walk to the hospitals; such as could not were taken upon stretchers from the places where they fell to selected points and thence the ambulances bore them, a miserable load, to their destination. Many were brought to the building, along the Taneytown Road, and too badly wounded to be carried further, died and were buried there, Union and Rebel soldiers together. At every house, and barn, and shed the wounded were; by many a cooling brook, or many a shady slope or grassy glade, the red flags beckoned them to their tented asylums, and there they gathered, in numbers a great army, a mutilated, bruised mass of humanity. Men with gray hair and furrowed cheeks and soft-lipped, beardless boys were there, for these bullets have made no distinction between age and youth. Every conceivable wound that iron and lead can make, blunt or sharp, bullet, ball, and shell, piercing, bruising, tearing, was there; sometimes so light that a bandage and cold water would restore the soldier to the ranks again; sometimes so severe that the poor victim in his hopeless pain, remedyless save by the only panacea for all mortal suffering, invoked that. The men are generally cheerful, and even those with frightful wounds, often are talking with animated faces of nothing but the battle and the victory. But some are downcast, their faces distorted with pain. Some have undergone the surgeon's work; some, like men at a ticket office, await impatiently their turn to have an arm or a leg cut off. Some walk about with an arm in a sling; some sit idly upon the ground;

some lie at full length upon a little straw, or a blanket, with their brawny, now bloodstained, limbs bare, and you may see where the minie bullet has struck or the shell has torn. From a small round hole upon many a manly breast, the red blood trickles, but the pallid cheek, the hard-drawn breath, and dim, closed eyes tell how near the source of life it has gone. The surgeons, with coats off and sleeves rolled up, and the hospital attendants with green bands upon their caps, are about their work; and their faces and clothes are spattered with blood; and though they look weary and tired, their work goes systematically and steadily on. How much and how long they have worked, the piles of legs, arms, feet, hands, and fingers about partially tell. Such sounds are heard sometimes — you would not have heard them upon the field — as evidence that bodies, bones, sinews, and muscles are not made of insensible stone. Nearby appear a row of small fresh mounds, placed side by side. They were not there day before yesterday. They will become more numerous every day.

Such things I saw as I rode along. At last I found the generals. General Gibbon was sitting on a chair that had been borrowed somewhere, with his wounded shoulder bare, and an attendant was bathing it with cold water. General Hancock was nearby in an ambulance. They were at the tents of the Second Corps hospitals, which were on Rock Run. As I approached General Gibbon, when he saw me, he began to hurrah and wave his right hand. He had heard the result. I said: "Oh, General, long and well may you wave" — and he shook me warmly by the hand. General Gibbon was struck by a bullet in the left shoulder, which had passed from the front through the flesh and out behind, fracturing the shoulder blade and inflicting a severe but not dangerous wound. He thinks he was the mark of a sharpshooter of the enemy hid in the bushes, near where he and I had sat so long during the cannonade; and he was wounded and taken off the field before the fire of the main lines of infantry had commenced, he being at the time he was hit near the left of his division. General Hancock was struck a little later near the same part of the field by a bullet, piercing and almost going through his thigh, without touching the bone, however. His wound was severe, also. He was carried back out of range, but before he would be carried off the field, he lay upon the ground in sight of the crest, where he could see something of the fight, until he knew what would be the result.

And then, at General Gibbon's request, I had to tell him and a large voluntary crowd of the wounded who pressed around now, for the wounds they showed not rebuked for closing up to the generals, the story of the fight. I was nothing loth; and I must say though I used sometimes before the war to make speeches, that I never had so enthusiastic an audience before. Cries of "good," "glorious," frequently interrupted me, and the storming of the wall was applauded by enthusiastic tears and the waving of battered, bloody hands.

By the custom of the service, the general had the right to have me along with him, while away with his wound; but duty and inclination attracted me still to the field, and I obtained the general's consent to stay. Accompanying General Gibbon to Westminster, the nearest point to which railroad trains then ran, and seeing him transferred from an ambulance to the cars for Baltimore on the 4th, the next day I returned to the field to his division, since his wounding in the command of General Harrow.

On the 6th of July, while my bullet bruise was yet too inflamed and sensitive for me to be good for much in the way of duty—the division was then halted for the day some four miles from the field on the Baltimore turnpike—I could not repress the desire or omit the opportunity to see again where the battle had been. With the right stirrup strap shortened in a manner to favor the bruised leg, I could ride my horse at a walk without serious discomfort. It seemed very strange upon approaching the horseshoe crest again, not to see it covered with the thousands of troops and horses and guns, but they were all gone—the armies, to my seeming, had vanished—and on that lovely summer morning the stillness and silence of death pervaded the localities where so recently the shouts and the cannon had thundered. The recent rains had washed out many an unsightly spot, and smoothed many a harrowed trace of the conflict; but one still needed no guide save the eyes, to follow the track of that storm, which the storms of heaven were powerless soon to entirely efface. The spade and shovel, so far as a little earth for the human bodies would render their task done, had completed their work—a great labor, that. But still might see under some concealing bush, or sheltering rock, what had once been a man, and the thousands of stricken horses still lay scattered as they had died. The scattered small arms and the accoutrements had been collected and carried away, almost all that were of any value; but great numbers of bent and splintered muskets, rent knapsacks and haversacks, bruised canteens, shreds of caps, coats, trousers, of blue or gray cloth, worthless belts and cartridge boxes, torn blankets, ammunition boxes, broken wheels, smashed limbers, shattered gun carriages, parts of harness, of all that men or horses wear or use in battle, were scattered broadcast over miles of the field. From these one could tell where the fight had been hottest. The rifle pits and epaulements and the trampled grass told where the lines had stood, and the batteries—the former being thicker where the enemy had been than those of our own construction. No soldier was to be seen, but numbers of civilians and boys, and some girls even, were curiously loitering about the field, and their faces showed not sadness or horror, but only staring wonder or smirking curiosity. They looked for mementoes of the battle to keep, they said; but their furtive attempts to conceal an uninjured musket or an untorn blanket—they had been told that all property left here belonged to the government showed that the love of gain was an ingredient at least of their motive for coming here. Of course, there was not the slightest objection to their taking anything they could find now; but their manner of doing it was the objectionable thing. I could now understand why soldiers had been asked a dollar for a small strip of old linen to bind their own wound, and not be compelled to go off to the hospitals.

Never elsewhere upon any field have I seen such abundant evidences of a terrific fire of cannon and musketry as upon this. Along the enemy's position, where our shells and shot had struck during the cannonade of the third, the trees had cast their trunks and branches as if they had been icicles shaken by a blast. And graves of the Rebels' making, and dead horses, and scattered accoutrements, showed that other things besides trees had been struck by our projectiles. I must say that, having seen the work of their guns upon the same occasion, I was gratified to see these things. Along the slope of Culp's Hill, in front of the position of the Twelfth, and the First Division of the First Corps, the trees were almost literally peeled, from the ground up some fifteen or twenty feet, so thick upon them were the scars the bullets had made. Upon a single tree not over a foot and a half in diameter, I actually counted as many as 250 bullet marks. The ground was covered by the little twigs that had been cut off by the hailstorm of lead. Such were the evidences of the storm under which Ewell's bold Rebels assaulted our breastworks on the night of the 2nd and the morning of the 3rd of July. And those works looked formidable, zig-zaging along these rocky crests, even now when not a musket was behind them. What madness on the part of the enemy to have attacked them! All along through these bullet-stormed woods were interspersed little patches of fresh earth, raised a foot or so above the surrounding ground. Some were very near the front of the works; and nearby, upon a tree whose bark had been smoothed by an axe, written in red chalk would be the words, not in fine handwriting, "75 Rebels buried here." "☞ 54 Rebs. there." And so on. Such was the burial and such the epitaph of many of those famous men, once led by the mighty Stonewall Jackson. Oh, this damned rebellion will make brutes of us all, if it is not soon quelled! Our own men were buried in graves, not trenches; and upon a piece of board, or stave of a barrel, or bit of cracker box, placed at the head, were neatly cut or penciled the name and regiment of the one buried in such. This practice was general, but of course there must be some exceptions, for sometimes the cannon's load had not left enough of a man to recognize or name. The reasons here for the more careful interment of our own dead than such as was given to the dead of the enemy are obvious and I think satisfactory. Our own dead were usually buried not long after they fell, and without any general order to that effect. It was a work that the men's hearts were in as soon as the fight was over and opportunity offered, to hunt out their dead companions, to make them a grave in some convenient spot, and decently composed with their blankets wrapped about them, to cover them tenderly with earth and mark their resting place. Such burials were not without as scalding tears as ever fell upon the face of coffined mortality. The dead of the enemy could not be buried until after the close of the battle. The army was about to move—some of it was already upon the march, before such burial commenced. Tools, save those carried by the pioneers, were many miles away with the train, and the burying parties were required to make all haste in their work, in order to be ready to move with their regiments. To make long shallow trenches, to collect the Rebel dead, often hundreds in one place, and to cover them hastily with a little earth, without name, number, or mark, save the shallow mound above them—their names of course they did not know—was the best that could be done. I should have been glad to have seen more formal burial, even of these men of the rebellion, both because hostilities should cease with death, and of the respect I have for them as my brave, though deluded, countrymen. I found fault with such burial at the time, though I knew that the best was done that could be under the circumstances; but it may perhaps soften somewhat the rising feelings upon this subject, of any who may be disposed to share mine, to remember that under similar circumstances—had the issue of the battle been reversed—our own dead would have had no burial at all, at the hands of the enemy, but, stripped of their clothing, their naked bodies would have been left to rot, and their bones to whiten upon the top of the ground where they fell. Plenty of such examples of Rebel magnanimity are not wanting, and one occurred on this field, too. Our dead that fell into the hands of the enemy on the 1st of July had been plundered of all their clothing, but they were left unburied until our own men buried them; the Rebels retreated at the end of the battle.

All was bustle and noise in the little town of Gettysburg, as I entered it on my tour of the field. From the afternoon of the 1st to the morning of the 4th of July, the enemy was in possession. Very many of the inhabitants had, upon the first approach of the enemy, or upon the retirement of our troops, fled their homes and the town not to return until after the battle. Now the town was a hospital where gray and blue mingled in about equal proportion. The public buildings, the courthouse, the churches and many private dwellings were full of wounded. There had been in some of the streets a good deal of fighting, and bullets had thickly spattered the fences and walls, and shells had riddled the houses from side to side. And the Rebels had done their work of pillage there, too, in spite of the smooth-sounding general order of the Rebel commander enjoining a sacred regard for private property—the order was really good and would sound marvelously well abroad or in history. All stores of drugs and medicines, of clothing, tinware, and all groceries had been rifled and emptied without pay or offer of recompense. Libraries, public and private, had been entered and the books scattered about the yards or destroyed. Great numbers of private dwellings had been entered and occupied without ceremony and whatever was liked had been appropriated or wantonly destroyed. Furniture had been smashed and beds ripped open, and apparently unlicensed pillage had reigned. Citizens and women who had remained had been kindly relieved of their money, their jewelry, and their watches—all this by the high-toned chivalry, the army of the magnanimous Lee! Put these things by the side of the acts of the "vandal Yankees" in Virginia, and then let mad Rebeldom prate of honor! But the people, the women and children that had fled, were returning, or had returned to their homes—such homes—and amid the general havoc were restoring as they could order to the desecrated firesides. And the faces of them all plainly told that with all they had lost and bad as was the condition of all things they found, they were better pleased with such homes than with wandering houseless in the fields with the Rebels there. All had treasures of incidents of the battle and of the occupation of the enemy—wonderful sights, escapes, witnessed encounters, wounds, the marvelous passage of shells or bullets which, upon the asking, or even without, they were willing to share with the stranger, I heard of no more than one or two cases of any personal injury received by any of the inhabitants. One woman was said to have been killed while at her washtub, sometime during the battle; but probably by a stray bullet coming a very long distance from our own men. For the next 100 years, Gettysburg will be rich in legends and traditions of the battle. I rode through the cemetery on "Cemetery Hill." How these quiet sleepers must have been astounded in their graves when the twenty-pound parrott guns thundered above them and the solid shot crushed their gravestones! The flowers, roses, and creeping vines that pious hands had planted to bloom and shed their odors over the ashes of dear ones gone, were trampled upon the ground and black with the cannon's soot. A dead horse lay by the marble shaft, and over it the marble finger pointed to the sky. The marble lamb that had slept its white sleep on the grave of a child, now lies blackened upon a broken gun-carriage. Such are the incongruities and jumblings of battle.

I looked away to *the group of trees*—the Rebel gunners know what ones I mean, and so do the survivors of Pickett's division—and a strange fascination led me thither. How thick are the marks of battle as I approach—the graves of the men of the Third Division of the Second Corps; the splintered oaks, the scattered horses—71 dead horses were on a spot some fifty yards square near the position of Woodruff's battery, and where he fell.

I stood solitary upon the crest by *the trees* where, less than three days ago, I had stood before; but now how changed is all the eye beholds. Do these thick mounds cover the fiery hearts that in the battle rage swept the crest and stormed the wall? I read their names—them, alas, I do not know—but I see the regiments marked on their frail monuments—"Twentieth Mass. Vols.," "Sixty-nine P. V.," "First Minn. Vols." and the rest—they are all represented, and as they fought commingled here. So I am not alone. These, my brethren of the fight, are with me. Sleep, noble brave! The foe shall not desecrate your sleep. Yonder thick trenches will hold them. As long as patriotism is a virtue, and treason a crime, your deeds have made this crest, your resting place, hallowed ground!

But I have seen and said enough of this battle. The unfortunate wounding of my general so early in the action of the 3rd of July, leaving important duties which, in the unreasoning excitement of the moment, I in part assumed, enabled me to do for the successful issue, something which under other circumstances would not have fallen to my rank or place. Deploring the occasion for taking away from the division in that moment of its need its soldierly, appropriate head, so cool, so clear, I am yet glad, as that was to be, that his example and his tuition have not been entirely in vain to me, and that my impulses then prompted me to do somewhat as he might have done had he been on the field. The encomiums of officers, so numerous and some of so high rank, generously accorded me for my conduct upon that occasion—I am not without vanity—were gratifying. My position as a staff officer gave me an opportunity to see much, perhaps as much as any one person, of that conflict. My observations were not so particular as if I had been attached to a smaller command; not so general as may have been those of a staff officer to the general commanding the army; but of such as they were, my heart was there, and I could do no less than to write something of them, in the intervals between marches and during the subsequent repose of the army at the close of the campaign. I have put somewhat upon these pages—I make no apology for the egotism, if such there is, of this account—it is not designed to be a history, but simply *my account* of the battle. It should not be assumed, if I have told of some occurrences, that there were not other important ones. I would not have it supposed that I have attempted to do full justice to the good conduct of the fallen, or the survivors of the First and Twelfth Corps. Others must tell of them. I did not see their work. A full account of *the battle as it was* will never—can never—be made. Who could sketch the changes, the constant shifting of the bloody panorama? It is not possible. The official reports may give results as to losses, with statements of attacks and repulses; they may also note the means by which results were attained, which is a statement of the number and kind of the forces employed, but the connection between means and results, the mode, the battle proper, these reports touch lightly. Two prominent reasons at least exist which go far to account for the general inadequacy of these official reports, or to account for their giving no true idea of what they assume to describe—the literary infirmity of the reporters and their not seeing themselves and their commands as others would have seen them. And factions, and parties, and politics, the curses of this Republic, are already putting in their unreasonable demands for the foremost honors of the field. "General Hooker won Gettysburg." How? Not with the army in person or by infinitesimal influence—leaving it almost four days before the battle when both armies were scattered and fifty miles apart! Was ever a claim so absurd? Hooker, and he alone, won the result at Chancellorsville. "General Howard won Gettysburg!" "Sickles saved the day!" Just Heaven, save the poor Army of the Potomac from its friends! It has more to dread and less to hope from them than from the red-bannered hosts of the rebellion. The states prefer each her claim for the sole brunt and winning of the fight. "Pennsylvania won it!" "New York won it!" "Did not old Greece, or some tribe from about the sources of the Nile win it?" For modern Greeks—from Cork—and African Hannibals were there. Those intermingled graves along the crest bearing the names of every loyal state, save one or two, should admonish these geese to cease to cackle. One of the armies of the country won the battle, and that army supposes that General Meade led it upon that occasion. If it be not one of the lessons that this war teaches, that we have a country paramount and supreme over faction, and party, and state, then was the blood of 50,000 citizens shed on this field in vain. For the reasons mentioned, of this battle, greater than that of Waterloo, a history, just, comprehensive, complete will never be written. By-and-by, out of the chaos of trash and falsehood that the newspapers hold, out of the disjointed mass of reports, out of the traditions and tales that came down from the field, some eye that never saw the battle will select, and some pen will write what will be named *the history*. With that the world will be and, if we are alive, we must be, content.

Already, as I rode down from the heights, nature's mysterious loom was at work, joining and weaving on her ceaseless web the shells that had broken there. Another spring shall green these trampled slopes, and flowers, planted by unseen hands, shall bloom upon these graves; another autumn and the yellow harvest shall ripen there—all not in less, but in higher perfection for this poured out blood. In another decade of years, in another century or age, we hope that the Union, by the same means, may repose in a securer peace and bloom in a higher civilization. Then what matters it if lame Tradition glean on this field and hand down her garbled sheaf—if deft story with furtive fingers plait her ballad wreaths, deeds of her heroes here? Or if stately history fill as she list her arbitrary tablet, the sounding record of this fight? Tradition, story, history—all will not efface the true, grand epic of Gettysburg.

Frank A. Haskell.
To H. M. Haskell.

COLOPHON

This edition of *The Battle of Gettysburg* was designed and set by Scott-Martin Kosofsky at The Philidor Company in Boston. The text typeface is Montaigne Sabon, designed by Mr. Kosofsky in 1993, based on the work of Jan Tschichold. The display types are Egiziano, Elephant, and Woodtype XXX Condensed. The book was created entirely in the PostScript language, on the Macintosh, using Quark XPress and Adobe Photoshop.